# Inspirational Blessings

## A Transformational Journey
## into Your Self

# Inspirational Blessings
## A Transformational Journey
## into
## Your Self

Nomi Sharron

BALBOA.
PRESS

A DIVISION OF HAY HOUSE

Balboa Press books may be ordered through booksellers or by contacting:

Balboa Press
A Division of Hay House
1663 Liberty Drive
Bloomington, IN 47403
www.balboapress.com
1 (877) 407-4847

Because of the dynamic nature of the Internet, any web addresses or links contained in this book may have changed since publication and may no longer be valid. The views expressed in this work are solely those of the author and do not necessarily reflect the views of the publisher, and the publisher hereby disclaims any responsibility for them.

The author of this book does not dispense medical advice or prescribe the use of any technique as a form of treatment for physical, emotional, or medical problems without the advice of a physician, either directly or indirectly. The intent of the author is only to offer information of a general nature to help you in your quest for emotional and spiritual well-being. In the event you use any of the information in this book for yourself, which is your constitutional right, the author and the publisher assume no responsibility for your actions.

Print information available on the last page.

ISBN: 978-1-5043-5870-5 (sc)
ISBN: 978-1-5043-5871-2 (e)

Library of Congress Control Number: 2016908800

Balboa Press rev. date: 12/21/2016

To my unseen Guides,
the lodestar of my life,
boundless gratitude
for being in the Blessings,
for being the Blessings,
for helping me to receive the Blessings
and understand their deeper meaning,
and for connecting me ever more profoundly
to the Divine within.
And thank you for blessing me
with your wisdom and inspiration,
your unconditional love,
and your humour!

∞

# Contents

∞

# Introduction

We have all been offered many more Blessings than we may have allowed ourselves to receive. Often we seem to be drowning in the noise and busyness of our hectic modern lives. We may be stressed at work, or struggling to juggle the demands of family and job. We may be stuck in the past, or wrapped up in making plans for the future. We do not see what the present is offering us. We don't have time to stop, time for ourselves; time to allow ourselves to receive our Blessings.

But it is not a lack of time that prevents us from receiving our Blessings. We do not hear the whispers, nor see the signs. We may be afraid, to look inside: afraid of what we may discover there; of what we may not discover there. Perhaps we don't feel very blessed. We may be ill, or perhaps our primary relationship is not going well; we may have lost our job, or our home, or someone close to us may have died. We may feel that life is a constant struggle. We look around and everyone else seems to be happy, prosperous and successful. But remember, our own life is the only one we see from the inside; what we see of other people's lives is only our projections. We may even feel that we do not deserve any better. But the man who moaned that he had no shoes, stopped moaning when he met someone who had no feet.

We are each offered many Blessings. But before we can receive them, we must make space for them by releasing whatever prevents us from being open to receive them: conditioned beliefs, certainties and assumptions; fears and self-doubt, anger, guilt, judgementalness and blame; feelings of isolation and alienation, a need to hide behind masks; and, controlling everything, our ever-present ego, constantly trying to dominate our lives. Our task is to work through these blocks and make space to receive our Blessings, allowing our life to unfold in its own way, without trying to manipulate it, or control it, or fix it.

Our Blessings are waiting for us to open up and receive them: waiting for the hunger in our heart to be stronger than the fear in our mind. Receiving is not passive. Rather it is a conscious act, being centred in the moment, fully present to ourselves and the world around us. Our Blessings connect us to the Source, to our own Higher Self, to the sacred. When we receive our Blessings, and manifest them in the physical world, we bring this sacredness into every aspect of our daily lives.

Our journey through life is a journey into healing – physical, emotional and spiritual; and our Blessings are the building blocks along this path. They provide us with nourishment and succour for the journey, helping us to integrate the fragmented and seemingly disparate parts of ourselves, showing us a way to reach balance and harmony, freedom, love, and peace. They reconnect us to the compassion of our heart, the yearning of our soul; to our integrity, our wholeness, our sense of belonging to the Oneness of the All That Is. Our Blessings are a key to expanding consciousness.

This book of Blessings is a guide for the journey, a blueprint for living your life with greater consciousness, bringing you more love, compassion, abundance and joy. It can help you to open your heart, and move towards that still place within where truth resides, allowing you to be alone in the stillness and silence, to connect to your Higher Self. Loving and nourishing yourself is not an indulgence; it is a spiritual imperative! For only by loving yourself unconditionally are you able truly to love others, live in caring relationships and nurture the planet.

Each Blessing is both the destination of your journey, and *the way you journey*. The goal and the way. It is important to remember this as you receive the Blessings; the destination you are seeking is the intention with which you invest the journey. The way *is* the goal. As you go through the Blessings, you will meet many spiritual paradoxes. They are each profoundly true, though perhaps you may not immediately understand them. Trust the gift of the paradox. Don't try to understand it with your mind. Know that your heart can hold truth that your mind cannot grasp.

Throughout the book, there are references to Spirit, God, the Source, the All That Is, the Divine. Feel free to use whatever term feels appropriate for you, for the Power beyond the physical. The names of God are not interchangeable, but they are all expressions of the same Oneness. The Blessings are written simply yet they are profound. Try to read them with your heart, as well as your head; to reach the wisdom and energy of each Blessing, beyond the words. Some words may be used in unexpected ways. Knowledge and knowing, for example, are not the same. 'Knowledge' refers to what we know with our minds; 'knowing' is the profound and unfathomable knowing of our heart.

All our Blessings are interconnected, and on the deepest level they are all one. Some truths are repeated, several times, in different Blessings: reminders of connections, or helping to strengthen your resolve when you might be questioning something that doesn't resonate with you. Don't dismiss your feelings, but try to stay with the Blessing: it may resonate with you differently on a further reading. There are many commas and short sentences, where you might not have expected them. This is intentional, to give you moments to pause and reflect, not to rush ahead; to stop, to breathe into the stillness and allow the energy of the Blessings, as well as the words, to seep into you.

Know that all your Blessings are inside you – all your Blessings. Remind yourself of this. Again. And again. This book offers you a portal into yourself, a key to unlock the door; tools to help you uncover, recover, discover, your Blessings; a transformational guided journey into your deepest Self. Call forth your Blessings; receive them, welcome them, celebrate them. Your Blessings are a refuge, a sanctuary, a place for you to gather strength and courage, wisdom and gratitude and love.

You may, of course, read the Blessings in any order you wish. But the first time you meet them, it is a good idea to go through them in the order in which they appear. This order represents a journey into your Higher Self, into the Divine deep within you, into the Mystery at the heart of the All That Is. The wisdom of many spiritual paths [for example, the Hindu and Buddhist knowledge of the Chakras, the Christian Sacrament, the Ten Sefirot of the Kabbalistic Tree of Life, the Shamanic Tower of Life] all suggest spiritual evolvement, from the basic physical needs of survival to the highest consciousness of immutable truth and our experience of the Divine.

The order of the Blessings loosely follows this journey. In the early stages, it offers Blessings that may be more easily accessible, such as curiosity, imagination, creativity; Blessings that perhaps you were 'helped' to lose touch with as a small child, but are now ready to receive. Blessings that appear in the latter part of the book, such as gratitude, humility, forgiveness, surrender, may be more difficult to receive if you haven't already journeyed through the earlier Blessings. There are fifty-two Blessings [plus the Joker, that has a special role!]. If you do decide to start by exploring the journey, you may like to stay with each Blessing for one week. This offers you a transformational year of journeying – plus extra time for the Joker! But spend as long or as little time with each Blessing as feels right for you. Honour your own intuition.

You may wish to journey through the Blessings once, or several times, and then use the Blessing Cards in any number of other ways [please see note below*** for information about the Blessing Cards]. However you choose to work with the Blessings, once you have been on the journey the Blessings will subsequently resonate with you more profoundly. Recognizing and receiving your Blessings brings with it profound knowing – and the unpredictable consequences of this. For knowing demands action – you cannot 'unknow' something because you do not wish to carry out the action. Making a commitment to explore and manifest your Blessings, does not give you extra Brownie points or currency with which to purchase future benefits! But it does offer a life fully lived and felt and experienced; a life lived in profound joy, love and ultimate freedom and peace. Manifesting our Blessings reminds us of who we are, all of who we are.

If you wish to undertake the journey of the Blessings, try to make a formal commitment with yourself to do this. This will give you discipline, and carry you through on lazy days, or days when you think you don't have time. [We can always find ten minutes! If you think you can't, your reluctance is not due to lack of time – however much it may seem to be – and you might want to look at this.]

The journey of the Blessings offers growing wisdom and compassion, and the recognition that our *life* is a Blessing. In each of us there is a yearning towards wholeness, freedom and peace. Our Blessings are a guide for the journey, expanding our consciousness, connecting us to our Higher Self and to the Source of the All That Is.

The journey into the Blessings is your journey home.

*"You are becoming more than the sum of your parts.*
*It is your time to wake up!"*
Saint Germain & Ashamarae McNamara:
The Blueprint of Oneness

*** The Blessing Cards are intended as an integral part of your Blessing journey, and if used with correct intention, will greatly enhance it. They are available in a beautiful Box Set, with a special instruction booklet giving guidance on the many ways to use them.
For details, please see page 132.

# Intimations of Immortality

Our birth is but a sleep and a forgetting:
The Soul that rises with us, our life's Star,
Hath had elsewhere its setting,
And cometh from afar:
Not in entire forgetfulness,
And not in utter nakedness,
But trailing clouds of glory do we come
From God, who is our home.

*From "Intimations of Immortality:*
*Recollections of Early Childhood"*

William Wordsworth

# Format of the Blessings and its Meaning

We are all blessed with manifold Blessings.
They are all within us.
But often we do not recognize or acknowledge them.

Our Blessings are waiting for us,
to grant us their wisdom, their Mystery, their meaning.

Each Blessing has the same format.
In the first part, we acknowledge and open ourselves up to receive the Blessing.
In the second part, we offer thanks for the help we are given
to receive and welcome this Blessing and manifest it in our lives.

In the second part of the Blessings, in those few words, "Thank you for helping me to..."
we express three profound truths:

* We acknowledge that we need help, but also that we need to take responsibility and do the work ourselves. [We ask for help, not for someone to do the work for us.]
* We acknowledge that help comes to us from a Higher Source.
* We express gratitude as we receive each Blessing. Gratitude is an intrinsic part of spiritual practice, opening us up to expanding consciousness, and to the Divine.

Moving more deeply into the paradox that is at the heart of spiritual truth, we accept that we need to take responsibility and do the work, but also we acknowledge that there is a Higher Power guiding our life, and we need to 'get out of the way', allowing ourselves to make space to receive all that we are offered.

As you open up to receive each Blessing,
focus on the Blessing being here and now.
Your Blessings are offered to you now,
in the present moment, this present moment – the only place to live.
You are blessed now.
And every now.
You are a Blessing.

∞

# Which Wolf Will You Feed?

One evening,
an old Cherokee told his grandson
about a battle that goes on inside people.
"My son," he said,
"The battle is between two wolves that live inside each of us.
One is Evil [Unhappiness].
It is anger, envy, jealousy, sorrow, regret, greed, arrogance,
self-pity, guilt, resentment, inferiority, lies,
false pride, superiority, and ego.
The other is Good [Happiness].
It is joy, peace, love, hope, serenity, humility,
kindness, benevolence, empathy, generosity,
truth, compassion, and faith."
The grandson thought about it for a minute
and then asked his grandfather:
"Which wolf wins?"
The old Cherokee smiled and replied simply,
"The one you feed."

*A Cherokee Indian Legend*

∞

# The Fifty-Two Blessings

1. I am blessed with the gift of starting the journey -
      - thank you for helping me to walk my path with openness, awareness, and trust

2. I am blessed with curiosity and wonder -
            - thank you for helping me to discover the wonders all around me

3. I am blessed with imagination -
                  - thank you for helping me to let it fuel everything I do

4. I am blessed with unfolding creativity -
      - thank you for helping me to recognize within me the creative energy of the Divine

5. I am blessed with spontaneity -
            - thank you for helping me to honour the promptings of this Blessing

6. I am blessed with a healthy body -
            - thank you for helping me to nurture it and understand its role in this life

7. I am blessed with touch -
                  - thank you for helping me to touch all beings with gentleness

8. I am blessed with sight and vision -
            - thank you for helping me to see with all my senses the signposts on the way

9. I am blessed with hearing and listening -
   - thank you for helping me to hear the silence of the universe, and the calling of my heart

10. I am blessed with the ability to provide for my physical needs -

    - thank you for helping me to do this without being acquisitive or greedy

11. I am blessed with sexual energy -

    - thank you for helping me to embrace this Blessing with integrity, honour and delight

12. I am blessed with a voice and words -

    - thank you for helping me always to speak directly from my heart

13. I am blessed with openness and flexibility -

    - thank you for helping me to be open to life and welcome change fearlessly

14. I am blessed with uniqueness -

    - thank you for helping me to accept and love the unique being that I am

15. I am blessed with beauty -

    - thank you for helping me to appreciate my inner and outer beauty

16. I am blessed with a smile -

    - thank you for helping me to spread joy with my smiles

17. I am blessed with intelligence -

    - thank you for helping me to use it wisely and dispassionately

18. I am blessed with discernment -

    - thank you for helping me to be discerning, and <u>not</u> judgemental

19. I am blessed with responsibility -

    - thank you for helping me to take responsibility for all aspects of my life

20. I am blessed with the gift of release -

    - thank you for helping me to let go of everything that keeps me stuck and fearful

21. I am blessed with acceptance -

    - thank you for helping me to accept what is, as it is

22. I am blessed with a sense of humour -

    - thank you for helping me to call on this frequently, lest I take myself, or others, too seriously

23. I am blessed with integrity -
    - thank you for helping me to manifest this Blessing in all that I am, all that I do

24. I am blessed with courage -
    - thank you for helping me to dare to take risks, and to welcome the unknown
    without fear

25. I am blessed with aspiration -
    - thank you for helping me to manifest this with integrity, compassion and ruth

26. I am blessed with mindfulness and awareness -
    - thank you for helping me to bring this Blessing into each present moment

27. I am blessed with intention -
    - thank you for helping me to focus my intention on the highest good of myself
    and others

28. I am blessed with happiness -
    - thank you for helping me to know that all happiness comes from within

29. I am blessed with abundance -
    - thank you for helping me to recognize my abundance in all things

30. I am blessed with generosity -
    - thank you for helping me to be generous to myself and others

31. I am blessed with compassion -
    - thank you for helping me to be compassionate towards myself
    and all sentient beings

32. I am blessed with the knowledge that I create my own reality -
    - thank you for helping me to create the reality envisioned by my Higher Self

33. I am blessed with living in the present moment -
    - thank you for helping me to know that this is the only place we can live

34. I am blessed with detachment -
    - thank you for helping me to let go of all attachment, all attachment

35. I am blessed with balance -

> > - thank you for helping me to be guided by the rhythms and harmony
> > of the universe

36. I am blessed with intuition and insight -

> > - thank you for helping me to recognize this voice of the Divine within me

37. I am blessed with dreams for my life's journey -

> > - thank you for helping me to follow them with imagination, tenacity, and courage

38. I am blessed with knowing ritual -

> > - thank you for helping me to celebrate in ritual more than my mind can grasp

39. I am blessed with healing -

> > - thank you for helping me to heal myself, and be a channel for healing others
> > and the planet

40. I am blessed with trust -

> > - thank you for helping me to trust the Divine unfolding of my life

41. I am blessed with the awareness of miracles -

> > - thank you for helping me to recognize their presence and invite them into my life

42. I am blessed with silence -

> > - thank you for helping me to be in the silence of the universe

43. I am blessed with help on my journey towards knowing myself -

> > - thank you for helping me along the way, to accept what I cannot know

44. I am blessed with unconditional love -

> > - thank you for helping me to love myself unconditionally, and the Divine
> > within all life

45. I am blessed with gratitude -

> > - thank you for helping me to live in gratitude for all that I am, all that I receive

46. I am blessed with humility -

> > - thank you for helping me to know my true worth, and so happily embrace humility

47. I am blessed with forgiveness -
- thank you for helping me to forgive myself, and those whom I feel have wronged me

48. I am blessed with consciousness -
- thank you for helping me to grow into awakened consciousness

49. I am blessed with surrender -
- thank you for helping me to surrender to Divine will

50. I am blessed with freedom -
- thank you for helping me to accept what is, and live in expanding freedom

51. I am blessed with prayer -
- thank you for helping me to know that my life is a prayer

52. I am blessed with the revelation of the Divine within me -
- thank you

The Joker: Thank you for helping me to take myself lightly

# A Return to Love

Our deepest fear is not that we are inadequate.
Our deepest fear is that we are powerful beyond measure.
It is our light, not our darkness, that frightens us.
We ask ourselves,
'Who am I to be brilliant, creative, talented, fabulous?'
Actually, who are you not to be?
We are meant to shine, as children do.
You are a child of God!
Your playing small doesn't serve the world.
There's nothing enlightened about shrinking
so that other people won't feel insecure around you.
We were born to make manifest
the glory of God that is within us.
It's not just in some of us: it's in everyone!
And as we let our own light shine
we unconsciously give other people permission
to do the same.
And as we liberate ourselves from our own fears,
our shining presence automatically liberates others.

*From "A Return to Love"*
Marianne Williamson

# The First Blessing

*I am blessed with the gift of starting the journey -*
*- thank you for helping me to walk my path with openness, awareness and trust*

Your journey starts here. Now. In this moment, as you become aware of it. Along the way many friends, many teachers, in many guises, may cross your path. They may be human, or animal, or anything within the natural world. They may come into your life for a moment, or stay for a lifetime. Welcome each one; they each have something to teach you, something to give you. And you have something to give them, too. Or they may be invisible guides, watching over you, offering you unconditional love and wisdom. Each life is a journey; a journey both to the Source, and to the sacred centre of our own being, deep within us. And of course, it is the same journey. Our yearning to connect to the oneness and unity of the All That Is, is our journey home.

Everything you need for your journey in this life is within you. Everything. Look within. As you consciously embark upon your journey, you invite the help you need to look inwards and find what is there. Observe. Each day brings a new beginning, new possibilities. The beauty that you see around you is a reflection of the beauty within you. Blessings and miracles strew your path. Notice them; they are there waiting for you to receive them. Receiving is not passive; it is a conscious act. 'Kabbalah' [the tradition of Jewish mysticism] is also the Hebrew word for 'receiving'. Being open to receive is the first lesson of the journey.

Be gentle with yourself as you move along your path. Accept what is there. You don't need to struggle to obtain, attain, retain anything. Once you stop struggling, you make space to experience your life as a Blessing. Allow your life to unfold in its own glorious way. Be present to the unfolding. Open your heart and embrace the wondrous adventures that are waiting for you. Receive with joy the wisdom that the universe offers you; learn to recognize what it has come to teach you. Don't chase after anything. All is as it is meant to be. Simply be, fully present, open and awake, in the moment, now – the only place where life can be lived. Let mystery and beauty and grace find you. You are not alone, ever. Venture forth with courage – you are the journeyer and the journey. Your journey is blessed.

*"The journey of a thousand miles begins beneath one's feet."*
*[popularly translated as "...begins with a single step."]*
Lao Tzu: The Way of Lao Tzu


*"This is the map of the inner universe, for the journey of life,*
*which is unknown, which is from now on..."*
Zen Master Hogen: On the Open Way


*"We are not human beings on a spiritual journey.*
*We are spiritual beings on a human journey."*
Yogi Bhajan, Founder of 3HO Foundation


*"Do not follow where the path may lead.*
*Go instead where there is no path and leave a trail."*
Ralph Waldo Emerson


*"The only impossible journey is the one you never begin."*
Anthony Robbins, author of self-help books


*"The longest journey is the journey from the head to the heart."*
Nomi Sharron: Paths to Spiritual Awakening

# The Second Blessing

*I am blessed with curiosity and wonder -*
*- thank you for helping me to discover the wonders all around me*

We are all born curious. As infants, we learn by following our curiosity. If we didn't, we would never learn to crawl, to walk or talk. In fact, we would probably not survive. Our experience as toddlers is driven by our curiosity, infused with fearlessness and our inability to understand risk. Our only boundaries are those imposed by others. Our curiosity is an on-going dialogue we have with the world around us, to see, to taste, to touch, to recognize, to know and understand; to discover how, and why, and what if…

As you have grown up, your curiosity may have been thwarted by the imposed limitations of others. But it is still there, an essential part of your being, waiting to be [re]discovered, [re]awakened, and celebrated. Your imagination and creativity and intelligence are all fuelled by your curiosity: to see something new, to reveal the hidden, to discover what was previously unknown, or unheard, or undreamt of. Let your curiosity drive you to explore new possibilities, to push out the boundaries of your experience and knowledge and wisdom. Discover the mystery of worlds within worlds; of tracing the opening of the tiniest flower, or the trajectory of the farthest star. Question everything. Answers lie in the awareness you invest in the quest.

Reconnect to your innate curiosity and sense of wonder. Set no limits. Be open to all its promptings, and don't judge. Follow it with passion, with tenacity, with a sense of adventure and fun; hold it in your grasp and don't let go. See the wonders all around you, unfettered by conditioning or fear. See with the eyes of a child, before 'reality' got in the way. Inhabit the hunger that drives you to know and discover and experience everything the universe offers. Allow it to take you to unfathomable places, to unseen worlds beyond the realm of the physical, to the mystical heart of the All That Is. Make no assumptions, take nothing for granted. This is the first step towards growing wisdom and self-empowerment – and an adventurous and exciting life!

*"'When you wake up in the morning...*
*What's the first thing you say to yourself, Piglet?'*
*I say, 'I wonder what's going to happen exciting today,' said Piglet."*
Benjamin Hoff: The Tao of Pooh


*"Curiosity is lying in wait to know every secret,*
*being open to understand every mystery."*
Ralph Waldo Emerson


*"Discovery consists of seeing what everybody has seen,*
*and thinking what nobody has thought."*
Albert Szent-Gyorgyi, Nobel Laureate in medicine


*"Millions saw the apple fall, but Newton asked why."*
Bernard Baruch, financier and philanthropist


*"My curiosity was interrupted by my schooling."*
George Bernard Shaw


*"I have begun to wonder if the secret of living well*
*is not in having all the answers,*
*but in pursuing unanswerable questions in good company."*
Rachel Naomi Remen: My Grandfather's Blessings

# The Third Blessing

*I am blessed with imagination -*

*- thank you for helping me to let it fuel everything I do*

Imagination is a truly miraculous Blessing. It has no limits. It can take us on marvellous adventures, to other worlds and other times. It can connect us to our highest aspirations and deepest yearnings. Our imagination fuels our curiosity, our sense of wonder, our inventiveness, and pushes us to reach for the stars. Our imagination lives in our Higher Self, feeding our creativity, and driving us to manifest our uniqueness, our spirit, all of who we are. Allowing our imagination to infuse everything we do expands all our experiences, and helps to make us whole.

Everything starts with imagination. Before we can manifest anything, we have to imagine it. So, imagine the life you would like to create, the reality you want to inhabit, the experiences you wish to have. Don't limit your imagination. Allow yourself to conjure and manifest the dreams that call to you from your deepest place of longing. Let go of the fear that holds you back, and know that deep within you live courage and moral strength. Your imagination can also help you to revive stagnant relationships, and find goodness and beauty in all those with whom you interact. See the world through the eyes of your imagination, and let it guide you to extend your humanity, to show compassion for yourself and others, and spread kindness and love.

Let your imagination fuel and enrich all your experiences; even the most mundane and routine activities can be transformed through imagination. Say 'yes' to promptings that liberate the longings of your heart, though you may not understand them. Think outside the box, feel beyond your boundaries, live creatively. Trust your imagination to lead you where it will. It comes from your Higher Self. Let it connect you to the Source, to the Great Creator. Let it transform hesitation into courage, fear into joy. Imagine the world beyond the physical and have the intention to recreate this around you. When you do this, the energy of the universe will help you. Ask yourself, frequently: What if…? How can I…? And, why not…? Your imagination is the voice of your heart and soul singing with delight. The more courageously you inhabit this Blessing, the more wondrous will be your experience of life. So, don the wings of your imagination and fly!

*"If you can imagine it, you can do it."*
Walt Disney


*"Logic will get you from A to Z.*
*Imagination will get you everywhere."*
Albert Einstein


*"Imagination is the eye of the soul."*
Joseph Joubert: Pensées


*"Imagination makes the impossible possible,*
*the possible probable,*
*and the probable inevitable."*
Many people have been credited with this quotation


*"A songbird doesn't sing because it has an answer.*
*It sings because it has a song."*
Maya Angelou


*"Achievement is only limited by imagination."*
A one-legged golf-player

# The Fourth Blessing

*I am blessed with unfolding creativity -*
*- thank you for helping me to recognize within me the creative energy of the Divine*

Creativity is our birthright, the Divine spark within us; we are all born creative beings. We are closest to God, the Great Creator, when we manifest our creativity. But often when we are children our creativity is kidnapped by adults with their own agendas. Sometimes it loses itself, unable to find its way home. Perhaps your creative attempts in childhood were ridiculed by others, and you have come to believe that you are not creative. But you *are*! We all are. Creativity is not the same as a particular talent: to write a best seller, compose great music or paint a masterpiece, though it may include any of these. Creativity is also about baking, gardening, sewing, making music, dancing, good conversation. It's about *how* we do, *whatever* we do; how we are. How we live. Intrinsically, creativity is an attitude to life, the way we live each moment, allowing our creative energy to flow untrammelled. We are most profoundly ourselves when we inhabit our creativity.

The journey of creativity is itself the goal and there is no destination. Creativity is about the journey of discovery; the *process,* not the outcome. It's time to let go of the inhibitions that limit us. They were formed by our conditioning, by other people's judgementalness; and by our own fears of inadequacy. They serve no purpose. So stop fretting about 'not being good enough'; this is a fiction of your mind. Stop worrying about what other people may think of your efforts; this is a fiction of their mind! Acknowledge your creativity, the key to a world of limitless possibilities, the most profound manifestation of who you are and what you are. Give yourself permission to truly inhabit your creativity – and surprise yourself!

Follow the calling of your creativity and recover, uncover, discover, your creative self. Set no limits; have no expectations, no attachment to outcome, no fixed idea of what the end result should be. Give yourself fully to the *process* of creating; of doing things for their own sake. For your own sake. Connect to the Divine within and allow yourself to be a vessel for the Great Creator to work through you, giving form to something that was without form, unmanifest. Bring your creative energy into the way you live your life, each moment. Allow the Divine creator within you to guide you and to enrich your life.

*"Every child is an artist.*
*The problem is how to remain an artist once you grow up."*
Pablo Picasso


*"The mind is not a vessel to be filled, but a fire to be kindled."*
Plutarch


*"I saw the angel in the marble and carved until I set him free."*
Michelangelo


*"Inside you there's an artist you don't know about...*
*Say yes quickly if you know,*
*if you've known it from before the beginning of the universe."*
Jelaluddin Rumi [13th century poet, scholar and Sufi mystic]


*"Our creative dreams and yearnings come from a Divine Source.*
*As we move towards our creative dreams,*
*we move towards our divinity."*
Julia Cameron: The Artist's Way


*"A friend asked me,*
*'Do you put yourself into your writing?'*
*'No, I don't. I find myself in my writing.'"*
Nomi Sharron

# The Fifth Blessing

*I am blessed with spontaneity -*
*- thank you for helping me to honour the promptings of this Blessing*

Our spontaneity is the expression of our choice to be who we are without the limitations imposed on us by others. It is the prompting of our heart's desire in any given moment. But sometimes, in our efforts to control our lives and the constant chatter of our minds, we may suppress our spontaneity. We see it as threatening; adding to our confusion, presenting too many possibilities, upsetting our routine and 'order'. But when we realize that we cannot control our lives, and we let go of the struggle, we allow the Blessing of spontaneity to flow freely through us. And it is indeed a wondrous Blessing, connecting us to our intuition and our Higher Self.

Being spontaneous does not mean being irresponsible. It means allowing yourself to go with the flow of life, without imposing restrictions. Spontaneity is a pure expression of who you are, your inner life force, not constrained by your busy mind and your ego. Allow your spontaneity to acknowledge the fluidity of life, the ebb and flow of the universe, the changing waves that are the only constancy. Hear within this the voice of your spontaneity calling you to follow your heart. Let your spontaneity lead you to manifest your creativity, and help you to recover buried dreams. Loosen the grip that entrenched patterns of 'sensible' behaviour may have on you. Don't let other people's judgements limit you. Allow yourself to live fully in the present moment, and let your spontaneity flourish. It is the prompting of the Divine within you. Trust it.

Celebrate your spontaneity by allowing these Blessings to flow untrammelled. Let your spontaneity open up your life experiences and free you from self-imposed limitations, and the limitations of others. Trust the insecurity of acting without predetermined plans, without certainties; this is 'creative insecurity' – and it is a wonderful Blessing! Live in your spontaneity. Welcome the unknown, and open the gates of your curiosity, your imagination, your creativity, with joyous expectation. Be brave! Move out of your comfort zone. Take risks, have adventures, delight in each moment. Step into the magical dance of a spontaneous life – and soar!

*"Only in spontaneity can we be who we truly are."*
John McLaughlin, guitarist and composer


*"Spontaneity is the quality of being able to do something*
*just because you feel like it, in the moment,*
*of trusting your intuition,*
*of taking yourself by surprise."*
Source Unknown


*"Do one spontaneous thing every day that scares you."*
Eleanor Roosevelt


*"Being spontaneous is being able to act with confidence,*
*trusting that you will have a positive experience*
*that will lead to greater self-awareness."*
Sylvia Clare: Trusting your Intuition


*"Say yes, and you'll figure it out afterwards."*
Tina Fey, Comedian / Actor


*"All growth is a leap in the dark,*
*a spontaneous unpremeditated act."*
Henry Miller

# The Sixth Blessing

*I am blessed with a healthy body –*
*— thank you for helping me to nurture it, and understand its role in this life*

In this life, we are blessed with a physical body. This, too, is a gift from the Divine. But 'we' are not our body, any more than we are our mind, or our emotions. They are each a part of us, but they do not define who we are. In this life, the role of our body is to ground us in the physical world. Our body is the temple of our soul, and needs to be honoured as such. But it also needs to be nourished for its own sake. We need to understand its role. As we move forward on our journey, we recognize that we are not our body, but rather the energy flowing through it. As we release the shackles of identification with the body, we move towards integration, wholeness and Self-realization.

Our physical body grounds us in the moment, the *only* place where life can be lived. By bringing our awareness into our body, we cannot *but* be in the present moment. We are not our body – we really have to take this on board! – but we need to recognize that it has its own intelligence, and much to teach us, if we are ready to learn. The body is a vessel for healing: symptoms of pain or disease in the body come to show us what ails us deep within, and so can lead us to healing the real causes of sickness, which are not in the body. The body has its own language, and also communicates to others. Be aware of what it is saying!

Ultimately, we need to transcend the body. But before we can do this, we need to accept it as it is: listen to it, nurture it, feed it healthy, life-affirming food, give it plenty of regular exercise. And stop criticizing it: too fat, too thin, ears too big, breasts too small… These judgements are fictions of your ego mind; let them go. Accepting your body, as it is, is a first step to accepting yourself, as you are, and it is hugely empowering. For those with a physical limitation, it may be more challenging. But many people with disabilities have extraordinary life-affirming stories, showing us all how courage and the human spirit can move beyond physical limitations. We are each unique. Honour your body, as it is. Care for its needs, without indulgence. The less attention it requires, the more time you have for your journey beyond the body, moving towards transcendence.

*"Do you not know that your body
is a temple of the Holy Spirit,
who is in you,
whom you have received from God?"*
The New Testament: 1 Corinthians 6, verse 19


*"Sickness is a defense against the truth."*
A Course in Miracles [Channeled Source]


*"Our own physical body possesses a wisdom
which we who inhabit the body lack."*
Henry Miller


*"Dance first.Think later.
It's the natural order."*
Samuel Beckett


*"This very body that we have...
is exactly what we need to be fully human,
fully awake, fully alive."*
Pema Chodron


*"Your body is the temple of your soul.
Honour it, and listen to its wisdom."*
Nomi Sharron: Tony Samara, A Modern Shaman… and Beyond

# The Seventh Blessing

*I am blessed with touch -*

*- thank you for helping me to touch all beings with gentleness*

The Blessing of touch is a shared Blessing; as it is given, it is also received. We become simultaneously the toucher and the touched. And maybe also the touch. Touch always speaks truth. It is more profound than words, which may change meaning from the lips of one to the ears of another. Loving touch is a shared moment, a connection of the heart between the one who gives and the one who receives. All beings long to be touched, caressed, hugged. Imagine a baby never being held; its growth would be stunted. We need loving touches at every age in order to thrive: the hand of friendship, a gentle caress, a spontaneous hug, an erotic touch. We may also touch people non-physically, touching hearts, with compassion, generosity, forgiveness, and love.

Touch can be a profound healer. For thousands of years, and in many traditions, touch has been known as an effective healer of disease and pain, and a source of life-giving energy. Massage is known to heal many ailments, as well as being a wonderful tonic. Touch may have immediate and also far-reaching effects. It can reach beyond the symptoms of the body, heal emotional distress, and re-align fractured parts of us, bringing us into healing and wholeness of body and spirit. And our touch may help others; connecting to the Divine within, we may also enable their healing. People living alone with pets they can cuddle are often less lonely, emotionally healthier, and happier than those without. Touch is "twice blessed", bringing healing and blessing to both giver and recipient.

Dismantle the protective wall you may have built to shield yourself from touch, out of fear of emotional exposure, vulnerability, or feelings of inadequacy. Be open to receive: a gentle touch from another can remind us that we are valued, and also empower the giver. Welcome intimacy into your life, but set healthy boundaries, not built on fear. Be generous with your touch. As you touch, so you are touched. Touch all beings with gentleness and compassion: people, animals, trees, plants, all living things. Let touch expand your heart, and remind you that you and all sentient beings are interconnected, part of the Oneness of all. Let your touch spread healing, harmony and love.

*"Touch comes before sight, before speech.*
*It is the first language,*
*and the last,*
*and it always tells the truth."*
Margaret Atwood


*"Too often we underestimate the power of touch...*
*which has the potential to turn a life around."*
Leo F. Buscaglia, professor and motivational speaker


*"I feel the healing hands of God*
*touch my heart and kiss my soul."*
Harley King, poet


*"Touch me. Remind me who I am."*
Stanley Kunitz, poet


*"Sometimes, reaching out and taking someone's hand*
*is the beginning of a journey."*
Vera Nazarian: The Perpetual Calendar of Inspiration


*"I want to touch the heart of the world*
*and make it smile."*
Charles de Lint, writer

# The Eighth Blessing

*I am blessed with sight and vision -*
*- thank you for helping me to see with all my senses the signposts on the way*

Each life is a journey. The way is open and accessible, mysterious and unknown. The signposts are there, to guide you. Notice them: with your eyes, your mind, your heart, your soul. Be open to see what is there: within you, in the world around you, and in the invisible worlds beyond. Let your vision be conscious, and not clouded by thoughts of what you think should be, nor by your expectations, assumptions or fears. Anything may be a sign to those who are willing to see: a butterfly crossing your path, an unusual cloud formation, the unexpected smile of a stranger. Take your time, and take in what is around you. What you see outside is simply a reflection of where you are on your journey.

You are blessed with the gift of sight and vision. Look outwards – and see the signposts showing you the landscape around you, gently guiding your journey forward. Don't rush ahead, following a pre-planned agenda, striving to reach your goal in a hurry. You have your whole life to journey, so move slowly. Give yourself time to receive the offerings of the universe, the miracles that strew your path. See with gratitude the beauty of the world around you: the perfection of nature, the blessings of Mother Earth. The farthest signposts may not be visible now. But as you move along your path, opening up with all your senses, they will appear. And you will be ready to recognize them when they do.

You are blessed with the gift of sight and vision. Look inwards, into the sacred core of your being – and see the love that is in your heart, the vision that your soul has brought with it for your journey in this life. Be guided by your Higher Self, and the wisdom of the Source. Notice the goodness and beauty in others, the truth behind the masks they wear, and reflect it back to them. See what they are hiding: the fear behind the arrogance, the sense of inadequacy behind the aggression. And don't be deflected from your path by others' blindness, or your own fear. See what is beyond the physical world; what is unknown, unformed, unmanifest. Open yourself up to experience the mysterious, the miraculous. See with all your senses. Celebrate your seeing, outwards, and inwards, and beyond…

*"The real voyage of discovery consists not in seeking new landscapes,*
*but in having new eyes."*
Marcel Proust


*"Reality exists behind our eyes,*
*not in front of them."*
Buddhist saying


*"I can see better when I close my eyes."*
Michael Bassey Johnson, writer


*"Without stirring abroad*
*one can know the whole world;*
*Without looking out of the window*
*one can see the way of heaven."*
Lao Tzu: Tao Te Ching


*"How alive is thought, invisible,*
*yet without thought there is no sight."*
Dejan Stojanovic: The Sun Watches the Sun


*"Vision is the art of seeing what is invisible."*
Jonathan Swift

# The Ninth Blessing

*I am blessed with hearing and of listening -*
*- thank you for helping me to hear the silence of the universe,*
*and the calling of my heart*

The universe speaks to us in many voices, but often we do not hear them. We are immersed in the constant buzzing in our heads, the noise all around us, the turmoil of our lives. The sounds of the universe – animal, plant, water, wind, air – are all around us; but they can reach us only in silence and stillness, not in a fanfare of noise. All the sounds, and the silence, of the universe are incorporated into the call of *aum*, the primordial sound of the universe. And all our Blessings are held within its vibrations. Chanting *aum* in meditation can open up our hearing and connect us to dimensions beyond the physical, offering us transformative energy of light and love, harmony and balance, healing and wholeness, uniting us in a higher consciousness of Oneness with the All That Is.

You are blessed with the gift of hearing. And of listening. They are not the same. Listening is a Blessing to be shared. Listening to others with your whole being is powerful and affirming, a healing Blessing for them – and also for you. Listen with your full attention, without interrupting with your own thoughts or ideas. And listen to the silences between their words, to what their hearts are saying, as well as their lips. Be fully present for them. Listen also to others who may seek your wisdom; we each have something to teach. And do not ignore the needs of those around you who do not speak, nor the distant cries of those far away who may need your help. Listen to those who do not ask, but may be in need of a loving friend.

You are blessed with the gift of listening. Listen to the voice of the Divine within you. It is your loadstar, guiding you to fulfil your mission on this earth. It lives within your Higher Self; recognize its immutable truth, trust its wisdom. Listen to the calling of your heart, and follow its guidance. Let it empower your journey. In the stillness and the silence, hear the unique sound of your soul, yearning to embrace the unity of the All That Is, to relinquish separateness, to connect with the Source. Listen to the voices that enrich your life and guide your journey home.

*"And He said,*
*Go forth and stand upon the mount before the Lord.*
*And behold, the Lord passed by,*
*and a great and strong wind rent the mountains,*
*and brake in pieces the rocks.*
*But the Lord was not in the wind.*
*And after the wind, an earthquake;*
*but the Lord was not in the earthquake.*
*And after the earthquake, a fire;*
*but the Lord was not in the fire.*
*And after the fire, a still small voice.*
*That was the voice of the Lord."*
The Old Testament: Kings 1, verse 19


*"Listening is such a simple act.*
*It requires us to be present...*
*Nothing else."*
Margaret J. Wheatly, writer and management consultant


*"The wise old owl lived in an oak;*
*The more he saw, the less he spoke;*
*The less he spoke, the more he heard;*
*Why can't we all be like that bird?"*
Edward H. Richards


*"The first duty of love is to listen."*
Paul Tillich, Lutheran theologian


*"The word 'listen' comprises the same letters as the word 'silent'."*
Alfred Brendel, pianist


*"We have each been given two ears and one mouth,*
*so that we may listen twice as much as we speak."*
Source Unkown

# The Tenth Blessing

*I am blessed with the ability to provide for my physical needs -*
*- thank you for helping me to do this without being acquisitive or greedy*

In this life we journey through the physical plane as well as the spiritual. And of course, it is one journey, encompassing all that we are, on every level. As mature adults, we need to provide for our survival needs and for those dependent upon us. Spirituality is not passive; it is not sitting and waiting for 'God to provide'. It is accepting what is, and at the same time taking responsibility for our lives. The world does not owe us anything; nor, once we are adult, does anyone else. Being offered abundance by the universe is a Blessing, not a right. We receive as we open ourselves up to allow our Blessings to reach us.

Money is a complicated issue and can buy many illusions. We need to examine our attitudes towards it honestly. What does money represent for you? Success? Status? Power? Control over others? Compensation for an emptiness within, a lack that can never be filled? Are you hooked on making more and more money, even though you have plenty? Are you envious of those who have more than you? Or do you find yourself despising affluence and pretending you do not want it because you feel impoverished? Perhaps you feel that you don't deserve more? You are not here to punish yourself. Living in material poverty is not of itself a virtue, although if deliberately chosen, with intention, poverty can be a transcendent spiritual choice. Material prosperity is not an evil, provided you come by it ethically. But recognize that money is a means, not a value.

Empower yourself by taking full responsibility for your needs, without expectations from others. Provide for those dependent upon you, but do not over-indulge children materially. They need your presence, not your presents. Be strong in your autonomy, your independence, but accept graciously what is freely given. Earn what you need, through work that is meaningful for you. Enjoy what you have and share freely with others. Be responsible towards those who may need your help, but offer support in a way that doesn't disempower them. Give what you can to those in need whom you don't know, through charitable organizations. Create a consciousness of abundance and sharing, and encourage others to do likewise. But remember, the real riches of your life are within you.

*"God helps those who help themselves."*
Algernon Sydney: 1698 article, Discourses Concerning Government


*"I am a magnet to prosperity in every area of my life.*
*I am open and receptive to all of it now."*
Many people have been credited with this quotation


*"If you give more focus on what you have and build your self-esteem,*
*you won't be so obsessive about money –*
*and maybe that is the beginning of real wealth."*
Dorothy Rowe: The Real Meaning of Money


*"I would rather be able to appreciate things I cannot have,*
*than to have things I am not able to appreciate."*
Elbert Hubbard, 19th century writer and publisher


*"All the money you make will never buy back your soul."*
Bob Dylan

# The Eleventh Blessing

*I am blessed with sexual energy -*
*- thank you for helping me to embrace this Blessing with integrity, honour and delight*

Our beliefs about sexuality create the way we experience it, just as our beliefs about everything create the reality we experience. Sometimes, when we embark upon our spiritual journey, we may feel that we should 'rise above' our bodies and deny our sexuality; that there is something 'impure' about sex. And, indeed, celibacy may be a valid choice, if it is made with the conscious intention of transcending physical desire, not suppressing it. But our sexuality is also a sacred Blessing, and how we choose to express it is also part of our spiritual journey. If we are stuck in rigid beliefs of religious 'morality' of sin and punishment, or if we are indulging in promiscuous sex to prove how free we are, we are not expressing our sexuality authentically. We need to examine our beliefs.

Our beliefs, about everything, keep us stuck in the fiction we are writing with our lives. It's time to let go of conditioned beliefs, or a desire to react against them, and find the place of your own integrity within yourself. Every Blessing given to us in this life comes from the Divine. Sexuality is a Blessing to be celebrated, not with license, but consciously chosen, as an authentic expression of your most loving and joyous and awake self. Expressing sexuality with integrity, in a deeply committed relationship, is also part of living a spiritual life. Sexuality is, of course, about much more than the body; it has physical, emotional and spiritual components. Lovemaking between two people who love each other deeply can be a profound spiritual experience, transcending the physical and reaching mystic union.

We express our sexual energy not only in our intimate relationships, but also in our creativity, our work; in the passion and joy with which we invest every aspect of our lives. It imbues our life force with vitality and feeds the energy that we bring to all our activities. Be comfortable in your body, but not overtly sexual; this is just a show. Move confidently, naturally, with grace. Look directly into people's eyes, smile, connect. Don't get caught up in playing games; this hides the real you and diminishes your integrity. Celebrate all aspects of your life with love, passion and delight.

*"Sacred sexuality acknowledges that our life force
and our sexual energy come from the same Source.
It is a profound expression of awe and wonder
that transcends any particular culture."*
Deborah Taj Anapol, clinical psychologist, columnist


*"I am convinced that life in a physical body
is meant to be an ecstatic experience."*
Shakti Gawain


*"When we touch the place in our lives
where sexuality and spirituality come together,
we touch our wholeness and the fullness of our power..."*
Judith Plaskow: Standing Again at Sinai – Judaism from a Feminist Perspective


*"When we practise sacred sexuality
we are working with cosmologically rooted principles,
balancing within ourselves
the heavenly yang [masculine energy] of the universe,
with the all-knowing, life-giving yin [feminine energy] of the earth."*
John Maxwell Taylor: Eros Ascending –
The Life-Transforming Power of Sacred Sexuality


*"It was not that we denied God,
but rather that we found Him in places
where He might have blushed to be."*
Nomi Sharron: Then Let the Barrier Fall

# The Twelfth Blessing

*I am blessed with a voice and words -*
*- thank you for helping me always to speak directly from my heart*

Language is a gift that blesses us, and enables us to bless others. It gives us a tool to name and clarify our thoughts, ideas and feelings, without 'fudging'; we cannot properly examine anything that remains amorphous and vague. Language can help us to articulate, to ourselves and to others, the process of becoming who we are, and give words to the story we are telling with our lives. With our voice we can communicate with others, and claim our place in the world. Words have their own power, and can express and change the way we experience the world. Language is also the medium of books, and reading inspirational books can help us to open our minds, develop our intellect, and move forward on our spiritual path.

Use your voice to speak your truth, and don't be deterred by others' opinions or judgements. Choose your words wisely, words that come from your highest integrity, your wholeness. Communicate directly with others. Say what you mean, and mean what you say. Don't hide behind clever words. Create a positive vocabulary that is life-affirming; for example, 'challenge' instead of 'problem', 'opportunity to explore the new' instead of 'fear of the unknown'. Create a positive way of seeing the world, and so help to manifest this reality. Help others by speaking words of encouragement, compassion and comfort. If you are ever tempted to speak negatively about anyone, or to gossip – don't! And don't listen to others' gossip. Strive to be impeccable in your word.

Words have power. Write your life with words of acceptance and affirmation, gratitude and humility, compassion and prayer. Discover the voice of your imagination, your creativity, your spontaneity and your dreams; your voice for making music and poetry and laughter. Speak gently, never with aggression; use words that spread wisdom, harmony and feelings of well-being. Use your voice to reach out to the Oneness of the All That Is, a conscious expression of your connection to the Source, which knows no separation. Let your words ring out from your heart, nourishing you and radiating joy and gratitude to those around you. Let your voice be an instrument for the Divine to work through you, spreading love, light and peace.

*"In the beginning was the Word,*
*and the Word was with God,*
*and the Word was God,"*
The New Testament, The Gospel According to St John: Chapter 1, verse 1


*[Before you speak, ask yourself:]*
*"Is it kind? Is it true? Is it necessary?*
*Does it improve upon the silence?"*
Sri Sathya Sai Baba


*"When the whole world keeps silent,*
*even one voice becomes powerful."*
Malala Yousafzai [Nobel Peace Prize Laureate, aged 17]


*"Do not follow the ideas of others,*
*but learn to listen to the voice within yourself."*
Zen Master Dogen


*"On the last day, say something beautiful,*
*or remain silent."*
The Koran


*"Only in silence may we hear the voice of our own divinity."*
Nomi Sharron: Paths to Spiritual Awakening

# The Thirteenth Blessing

*I am blessed with openness and flexibility -*
*- thank you for helping me to be open to life and welcome change fearlessly*

Receiving and manifesting this Blessing can change our life in wondrous ways. Being open and flexible helps us to let go of the limitations we create for ourselves, and push out our boundaries. It can free us from rigid patterns of thought and behaviour, fixed ideas, assumptions, and beliefs that keep us stuck in old paradigms, thus opening us up to explore new horizons. Embracing this Blessing can help us to let go of our need for certainty and predetermined outcomes, move beyond our wish to control life, and accept what is. It can strengthen our resolve to journey forward bravely into the unknown. Life is changing all the time. Each day brings new possibilities; each moment offers new wisdom and understanding. The only constant in life is change.

Be courageous and move beyond the safety of the familiar. Examine the ways in which your behaviour follows a fixed routine. Dare to change it, to break out of the confines of your comfort zone, and discover new ways of seeing, of doing. Push out the boundaries of what you allow yourself to attempt. Let go of the script in your head that dictates pre-programmed reactions, and move into unchartered waters. Let yourself be surprised! Connect to your spontaneity and follow its lead. Live fully present in each moment, with all the openness of your life force. Gird your loins and welcome new experiences with joy. Meet the challenges of the unknown with a sense of excitement and wonder.

Today, do something different, and break your addiction to your routine. Eat a different food, take a different route to work, wear something you wouldn't normally wear. Let go of the automatic pilot inside your head, your investment in your certainties, your pre-programmed responses to people and situations. Make space in your head for new ways of seeing the world. Make space in your heart to embrace what is, in the present moment. Remind yourself that you have the courage to confront your fear of change. Manifest this Blessing as you move along your spiritual path, welcoming the surprises along the way. They all have something to teach you. Go with the flow, be open and receptive to everything the universe offers you. Feel your life enhanced and enriched beyond measure.

*"If we are only open
to that which accords with what we already know,
We might as well stay shut."*
Alan Watts


*"The measure of intelligence is the flexibility to change."*
Albert Einstein


*"The mind is like a parachute.
It only functions when it's open."*
Finley Peter Dunne, writer and humourist


*"The time comes when the risk it takes
to remain tight in the bud
is more painful
than the risk it takes to blossom."*
Anais Nin


*"Openness, patience, receptivity, solitude, is everything."*
Rainer Maria Rilke


*"The boldness of asking deep questions
requires unforeseen flexibility
if we are to accept the answers."*
Brian Greene, theoretical physicist

# The Fourteenth Blessing

*I am blessed with uniqueness -*
*- thank you for helping me to accept and love the unique being that I am*

Before we are born our soul chooses its mission in this life, and the lessons it seeks to learn. In order to accomplish this, it chooses the family into which it will be born, the place, the culture, etc. And many factors influence who we become: the time of our birth and the astrological combination, our position within the family, the needs of our parents, the love we receive, or don't receive, as children; the religion and societal norms into which we are born. We each also bring with us into the world our own uniqueness and karma. Our journey is to discover and fulfil the mission of our soul.

Our path in this life is ours alone, and no-one else can walk it for us. But as children, we are often 'put into boxes', and our uniqueness is not recognized. Now it is time to allow your uniqueness to blossom, to be true to yourself. Learn to see and accept yourself as you are, without pretence, without masks. And accept what you perceive as your 'flaws'; these are tools for learning about yourself, for gaining wisdom and moving forward. Don't be blown off course by other people's judgementalness. Nor your own. And don't compare yourself to others, for you will always find yourself wanting: you are not 'as clever as… as successful as… as creative as…' No, nor are you meant to be. But are you as clever, as successful, as creative, as *you* can be?

We are all offered similar Blessings, but we each receive them [or don't receive them] in our own unique way. The way you receive your Blessings paves your spiritual path. Be open to receive. Fulfil your own potential, your vision for this life, your dreams and yearnings. Expand your horizons, being and becoming. Embrace your Higher Self and act from your own integrity. Don't be swayed by others' agendas, or by what others may think of you. Be true to your own values, trust your intuition, stand up for what you know to be right. Your journey in this life is unique. Only you can fulfil its purpose. If you don't fulfil it, it will not be fulfilled. Not for you – and not for the world. What an awesome responsibility! And how empowering! Honour your uniqueness. Be the best that you can be. It is enough.

*"Look within, thou art the Buddha."*
Buddha


*"What makes you different, makes you beautiful."*
Source Unknown


*"When I let go of what I am,*
*I become what I might be.*
*When I let go of what I have,*
*I receive what I need."*
Lao Tzu


*"When Piedro died...*
*and was asked by the Creator of All*
*to give an account of his life,*
*he said sadly:*
*'I was just a simple shoemaker.*
*I was not as noble as my father,*
*nor as wise as the village chief.*
*I was not as gentle as my mother,*
*nor as clever as my brother.*
*Nor was I as rich in good deeds as my beloved wife.'*
*The Creator of All smiled gently, and said:*
*'I have just one question for you.*
*Were you as noble, as wise, as gentle, as clever,*
*as rich in good deeds,*
*as Piedro could have been?'"*
Nomi Sharron: Piedro's Story

# The Fifteenth Blessing

*I am blessed with beauty -*

*- thank you for helping me to appreciate my inner and outer beauty*

This Blessing teaches us what beauty really is – and what it is not. Beauty is not about a pretty or handsome face. Nor is it the touched-up photograph of a model in a glossy magazine. Trying to fit into a society's 'ideals' of beauty is a nonsense, and is also culturally specific: there are societies, for example, that regard fat as beautiful, and thin as decidedly unhealthy. And beauty has nothing to do with age. A woman of fifty, truly loving herself, and comfortable in her body, may be more beautiful than a skinny twenty-five-year-old trying to be someone she's not. A man of sixty, with a deeply weathered face, may manifest beauty through eyes that are alive and alert, and a smile that radiates warmth.

We are each beautiful in our own unique way. This Blessing comes to you as a celebration of *your* beauty. Recognize it, inhabit it, honour it. Accept yourself as you are, without judgement or criticism, and without comparison to others. Acknowledge what makes you beautiful: a joyous heart, a loving smile, a body at ease with itself; a face glowing with life and energy. But your beauty is much more profound than this. It is the beauty of your soul, connected to the All That Is, the unity and wisdom of the Source; a soul living in balance and harmony, at peace with itself and the universe. Embrace your beauty – body, mind, heart and soul. Live fully in the moment, pulsating with life and vitality, emanating light and energy and the joy of being alive. See your beauty mirrored back to you in the eyes of those around you.

This Blessing is a celebration of beauty in all its manifestations. Recognize the true beauty of others and reflect it back to them. This helps them to inhabit their own beauty, and in turn to reflect the beauty of others back to them. See the beauty in the perfection of Creation – in all living beings that walk, crawl, fly, swim or stand; the glory of a sunset, the power of a thunderstorm, stars lighting up the night sky. You are a mirror of the beauty around you, just as the beauty of Creation mirrors your beauty. Allow yourself to be touched and enriched and ennobled by the infinite guises of beauty, within, without, and beyond…

*"All the wonder you have ever beheld*
*is an expression of your beautiful self."*
Saint Germain & Ashamarae McNamara: The Blueprint of Oneness


*"'Beauty is truth, truth beauty' – that is all*
*Ye know on earth, and all ye need to know."*
John Keats: Ode on a Grecian Urn


*"Think of all the beauty still left around you and be happy."*
Anne Frank: The Diary of Anne Frank [written aged 13, in hiding from the Nazis]


*"Beauty is not in the face;*
*beauty is a light in the heart."*
Kahlil Gibran


*"People are like stained-glass windows.*
*They sparkle and shine when the sun is out.*
*But when darkness sets in,*
*their true beauty is revealed only if there is a light from within."*
Elizabeth Kubler-Ross


*"Remember, wrinkles are places where smiles have lived!"*
Nomi Sharron: Paths to Spiritual Awakening

# The Sixteenth Blessing

*I am blessed with a smile -*

*- thank you for helping me to spread joy with my smiles*

Like touch, the Blessing of a smile is a shared Blessing. It is given, but it is not given away. It stays to bless the giver too. Our smile is an expression of our joy in the moment. It is impossible to feel tense, angry, resentful or depressed when you smile. [Try smiling and feeling any negative emotion at the same time. It can't be done!] Smiling relaxes the face and jaw, and actually triggers the release of endorphins, which add to feelings of well-being. A smile can calm a fraught situation, diffuse tensions, halt an argument, overcome divisions and win over adversaries. What an amazing Blessing in such a simple act!

All our Blessings help us to receive love, joy and healing. But our smile can also bring these Blessings to others. Our smile is a Blessing from us to those around us, a wordless communication of our delight in seeing them. Smiles come from the heart, not just the lips. And they are infectious. When you smile to others, they generally smile as well; they will feel better for it, and so will you. So you create a virtuous circle of Blessing, a gift that you give to others, without relinquishing it. You increase your own pleasure, as well as that of those who receive it. A smile lights up your face, and reflects light to others, spreading joy in a world that is thirsty for joy.

Next time you feel angry, frustrated or disgruntled – try smiling. Better still, smile into the mirror, and share your smile with the beautiful calm person smiling back to you. If you encounter someone who is hostile or acting out, smile to them, instead of getting caught up in their drama. Smile for no reason, just to express your delight in the moment, in being alive. Spread smiles around you, to those you know and love, and bring them joy. And today, smile to a stranger, who may smile to another stranger, who may smile… You will feel good, and who knows, perhaps you will start a chain reaction of smiles that will ripple outwards across the world, increasing the abundance of well-being, unity and joy.

*"A smile is the light in the window of your face
that tells others you're at home."*
Denis Waitley


*"Sometimes your joy is the source of your smile,
but sometimes your smile can be the source of your joy."*
Thich Nhat Hanh


*"Let my soul smile through my heart
and my heart smile through my eyes,
that I may scatter rich smiles in sad hearts."*
Paramahansa Yogananda


*"Don't cry because it's over.
Smile because it happened."*
Dr. Seuss


*"Let your smile be a rainbow in someone else's cloud."*
Maya Angelou


*"Peace begins with a smile."*
Mother Teresa

# The Seventeenth Blessing

*I am blessed with intelligence –*

*– thank you for helping me to use it wisely and dispassionately*

Intelligence is a powerful Blessing. It is the instrument of our logical mind, the tool of our reason, the expression of our cognitive power, the home of our intellectual acuity; it helps us to evaluate ideas and is the conduit of our memory. Philosophers talk of an unexamined life as an impoverished one. Our intelligence helps us to examine our life, to evaluate the results of our decisions and learn from our 'mistakes'. It can help us to acquire and discern the value of knowledge from the vast field of learning available in the post-modern era. It may help us to take responsibility for our lives as mature adults. Our intelligence is a bridge from our inner self to the outer world.

Intelligence is a wonderful Blessing – as long as we understand its place in our life, and do not inflate its importance. Use it to clarify your thoughts, to question inherited or conditioned beliefs, certainties and perceptions, and to challenge all assumptions. Use it to understand your need for the dramas you create, and extricate yourself from their influence. Let your intelligence help you to clear muddied waters and untie the knots that bind you. Use it to understand the manipulations of the world and the demands of the prevailing culture. Have the courage to see things differently, and be guided by your own discernment. Simplify your life. Be savvy to what is beneath the surface of other people's talk and behaviour, and express yourself directly and honestly in all your interactions with others. Used wisely and incisively, and unfettered by emotional baggage, your intelligence can be a formidable tool.

But your intelligence does not define you. You are much more than this. Remind yourself that your intelligence is one of your many Blessings. Trust it to guide your intellectual curiosity, to bring clarity to your thoughts, your decisions and your actions. Be open to its power and let it empower you, but do *not* let it control you. And be mindful that your intelligence can also be a tool of your ego, cleverly manipulating you in order to keep you safely within its domain, and convince you that the world it creates is reality. But it is not. So beware! And be aware. You have many Blessings to guide you on your journey in this life. A clever mind is a wonderful gift, but it is no substitute for a wise heart. Let your intelligence be a useful and efficient servant, not a tyrannical master.

*"It takes something more than intelligence to act intelligently."*
Fyodor Dostoevsky: Crime and Punishment


*"Intelligence with Deity can lead to greatness.*
*Intelligence without Deity*
*partners the twins ignorance and arrogance."*
Damon Thueson, firearms instructor and religious believer


*"The ability to observe without judging*
*is the highest form of intelligence."*
Jiddu Krishnamurti


*"I know that I am intelligent,*
*because I know that I know nothing."*
Socrates


*"Intelligence is the ability to adapt to change."*
Stephen Hawking


*"Intellectuals solve problems.*
*Geniuses prevent them."*
Albert Einstein

# The Eighteenth Blessing

*I am blessed with discernment -*
*- thank you for helping me to be discerning and <u>not</u> judgemental*

The Blessing of discernment brings us conscious choice: in evaluating ideas and situations, in examining perceptions and opinions, and in questioning conditioned assumptions and beliefs, parental or societal. Discernment is often confused with judgement and it is crucial to know the difference. Judgement spreads negativity and adds to a culture of comparison and blame. It may harm the one who is judged, and harm those who do the judging by giving them a false sense of superiority. If we are ever tempted to judge others, we should look within ourselves and see where our judgementalness is coming from, and what lies behind it. Being judgemental is one of the biggest obstacles on our spiritual path and we need to be aware of this.

As well as being judgemental of others, many of us make a practice of judging ourselves, and finding ourselves wanting; we can never live up to the standards we set ourselves. Self-judgement brings up emotions of inadequacy, guilt and shame. It curbs our spontaneity, our creativity and imagination, and inhibits the flow of our life force. It blames us for making 'mistakes'. But mistakes are not negative; they are the way life teaches us. Judging them simply stops us from learning the lessons they bring us. So, banish judgementalness, and welcome your mistakes as teachers on your path. Be open, be discerning, learn their lessons, and move on. Stand back and observe your life. Discernment is knowing that judgementalness is not a Blessing! Ever. Discernment is seeing situations as they are, without emotional investment, and then making responsible choices: how you choose to see the world, and its infinite, complex and wondrous possibilities.

Use your discernment to question controlling behaviour, certainties, beliefs, assumptions and opinions – other people's, and your own. See each situation as it is, without colouring it with your expectations, your hopes, or your fears. Let all your decisions come from a place of discernment. This is the expression of your integrity, your authenticity, your wholeness; it empowers you and imbues you with feelings of rightness and well-being. Discernment can also help to bring wisdom and compassion to situations of injustice in the world, and show you the possibilities of alleviating suffering. Let your discernment guide and empower your life, bringing you a sense of contentment and peace. Show others what is possible, and be an example to the world.

*"Judge not, that ye be not judged."*
The New Testament: Matthew - 7.1


*"Take each man's censure,*
*But reserve thy judgement."*
William Shakespeare: Hamlet - Act 1, Scene 3


*"Let discernment be your trustee,*
*and mistakes your teacher."*
T. F. Hodge: From Within I Rise


*"Discernment is God's call to intercession,*
*never to fault-finding."*
Corrie ten Boom, Christian writer,
imprisoned in Holland for helping Jews to escape the Nazis


*"Every time you judge yourself,*
*you break your own heart."*
Swami Kripalvananda [quoted in Your Yoga Experience by Sandi Greenberg]


*"When you judge others, you do not define them,*
*you define yourself."*
Earl Nightingale, writer, known as the "Dean of Personal Development"

# The Nineteenth Blessing

*I am blessed with responsibility -*
*- thank you for helping me to take responsibility for all aspects of my life*

Growing up and becoming an adult means letting go of childhood 'baggage' and taking responsibility for our life now. Most of us have issues with our parents, even if they loved us. But however they behaved when we were children – whether they were neglectful, exploitative, or even abusive, or if they didn't 'recognize' us – we are now adults. And being an adult means accepting responsibility for ourselves. Blaming others for whatever we feel is wrong with our lives prolongs the power that they have over us, and keeps us stuck in 'victimhood'. We need to draw a line under the past and move on.

This Blessing brings us response-ability – the ability to respond in any situation. [Responding is not the same as reacting; responding is a conscious choice, reacting is automatic.] We alone are responsible for our choices. Taking responsibility does not mean trying to control our life, which is not possible. It means accepting what is, and then making responsible choices. Responsibility is not 'duty', which comes from a sense of obligation, and may be a burden; it is a choice that comes from our Higher Self. Responsibility should also govern your behaviour towards others. If people behave towards you inappropriately, tell them calmly how you feel, but don't act out your emotions. Having a temper tantrum is not an adult way to behave! If you feel angry, look at what this can teach you, then let it go. Don't take it out on anyone else. Remind yourself that no-one can 'make you' feel angry, or indeed anything else, though they may 'trigger' an emotion. It's really important to take this on board. *Only you are responsible for your emotions.* Take responsibility and own them.

Remember, other people behave towards you because of who *they* are, not because of who *you* are; their behaviour is their agenda. Be aware of this in your response to others, and in your own actions. *Act* from your own integrity and autonomy; don't *react* to others' behaviour towards you. Be responsible for your thoughts and feelings, as well as your actions. The profound meaning of this Blessing is to lead you towards real freedom. And the first step is to take full responsibility for every aspect of your life. Remember also that we are all responsible for nurturing the planet. Take care of Mother Earth, show her compassion and love, and enjoy her myriad Blessings in a responsible way.

*"Accept responsibility for your actions.*
*Be accountable for your results.*
*Take ownership of your mistakes."*
Source Unknown


*"I am responsible for myself.*
*Nobody else is responsible for me.*
*It is utterly my own responsibility."*
Osho: The Book of Wisdom


*"It is not only for what we do that we are held responsible,*
*but also for what we do not do."*
Jean Baptiste Poquelin Molière


*"When you take responsibility,*
*you take your life in your own hands.*
*And what happens?*
*A terrible thing: there is no-one to blame!"*
Erica Jong: Fear of Flying


*"It is not our abilities that show who we really are.*
*It is our choices."*
J.K. Rowling: Harry Potter and the Chamber of Secrets


*"I needed to do something that was not allowed."*
Erich Lichtblau [painting in his bunk at night,
under threat of death at Theresienstadt concentration camp during the Holocaust]

# The Twentieth Blessing

*I am blessed with the gift of release -*
*- thank you for helping me to let go of everything that keeps me stuck and fearful*

The beginning of all spiritual practice is letting go; letting go of who we are in order to become who we are meant to be. Our spiritual journey is not a quest for information, nor new ideas or beliefs, nor even knowledge. Rather, it is a process of letting go and making space to receive. We need to start the process of release – right now! To let go of everything that keeps us in our comfort zone, closed, afraid and stuck: our assumptions, opinions, expectations, and beliefs; the clutter and confusion and chaos that fill our mind; our dogmatism and self-righteousness; the dominance of our ego and our emotional investment in outcome. The tyranny of the past.

Wow! That is a lot to let go of! But it is old 'baggage'; we do no need it, and it is hampering our journey forward. We hang on to it because it is what we're used to, and familiarity is comforting. And because of fear. Behind all our resistance to letting go, lies fear; fear of embracing the unknown. Our fears imprison us. But they are illusions that our ego manufactures in order to keep us safe and stop us from taking risks. But 'safe' means limited, an impoverished life. When we are able to look within, to question how we are living, and let go of our props, a new world opens up before us, a new way of seeing, and experiencing, our life.

So, declutter your life! Start to relinquish the past, and the baggage that is weighing you down. Begin to unearth the fears that lie behind everything that keeps you stuck. Talk to them, name them, ask them questions. Be open to what comes up – you may surprise yourself! Start to dissolve them by giving them love. Each time you go through this process it will become easier, and you will reach more deeply into the cause of your fears. This will also help you to stop struggling to control life – it is not yours to control. Connect to your heart, and release everything that impedes your spiritual journey. Relinquish what was, and make space to welcome what is. Greet the unknown with courage. Let go, release, again, and again; it's an on-going process and there is always more work to do... So start now! Doff the clothes of your slavery to the past, and embrace the extraordinary, rich and rewarding adventure that your life is meant to be.

*"Let go of what was.*
*Surrender to what is.*
*Trust in what will be."*
Sonia Ricotti: Unsinkable: How to Bounce Back Quickly
When Life Knocks You Down


*"Fear changes to love*
*when you walk through it and release it."*
Mavis Meaker, Spiritual Guide


*"In the end, just three things matter:*
*How well we have lived,*
*how well we have loved,*
*how well we have learned to let go."*
Jack Kornfield


*"Let the senses go.*
*Let desires go.*
*Let conflicts go.*
*Let ideas go.*
*Let the fiction of life and death go.*
*Just remain at the centre, watching.*
*And then forget that you are there."*
Lao Tzu: Hua Hu Ching


*"Stand tall and proud,*
*wise and grounded, like a tree.*
*Shed your leaves when you no longer need them*
*and make space for new growth."*
Nomi Sharron: Paths to Spiritual Awakening

# The Twenty-First Blessing

*I am blessed with acceptance -*

*- thank you for helping me to accept what is, as it is*

The Blessing of acceptance may seem simple, but it is a profound spiritual Blessing, and is essential for all change. It is the beginning of spiritual growth, both an instrument and a marker of our evolvement. Acceptance means accepting what is, and recognizing that we cannot control life. Our first task is to accept ourselves, as we are, with all our perceived 'flaws' and 'failings'. These are simply an illusion of our perception, and when seen with awareness, they dissolve. Accepting ourselves, as we are, means letting go of self-criticism, shame and guilt, and welcoming the way our life unfolds, even if we don't understand it. It means accepting ourselves, accepting others, accepting the universe, as we each are, and moving with the flow of life.

Accepting this Blessing can change our life. It frees us from the burden of judgementalness and blame, among the greatest stumbling blocks on our spiritual path. Accepting others as they are, recognizing that each person is unique, with his / her own path to walk, is a fundamental tenet of the spiritual way. Don't try to change anyone [not even your partner; especially not your partner!]. This is arrogant and also a waste of time; you cannot change anyone else. You can teach by example; acting with integrity, manifesting compassion and love. At the same time, you need to accept that others may not follow your example; this is their choice and nothing to do with you. Ironically, perhaps, by accepting others, you connect more deeply to your own integrity.

Remind yourself that you are created in the image of God and are a manifestation of Divine perfection. Accept this, even though you may not know its purpose. Accept your life, as it is, as it unfolds. Don't try to fight it, for it's not your enemy. Don't try to fix it, for it's not broken. And don't try to control it, for you cannot! Simply accept it. And accepting your life includes accepting the universe, without preconceived ideas of what should be. It is perfect as it is, the manifestation of God's will, just as your life unfolds as the will of God. Be in the unfolding; enjoy what each moment offers you. Accept what is and open yourself up to receive. Celebrate the flow of your life, as it is. Live in acceptance and allow grace to find you.

*"God grant me the serenity to accept the things I cannot change;*
*the courage to change the things I can;*
*and the wisdom to know the difference."*
Reinhold Niebuhr, American theologian and philosopher: The Serenity Prayer


*"We cannot change anything unless we accept it.*
*Condemnation does not liberate, it oppresses."*
Carl Gustav Jung: Modern Man in Search of a Soul


*"I can't change the direction of the wind,*
*but I can adjust my sails to reach my destination."*
Jimmy Dean, country music singer


*"Understanding the power of acceptance*
*is the only way to find peace and heal."*
Rachel Naomi Remen: My Grandfather's Blessings


*"Acceptance does not mean resignation, which is giving in.*
*Acceptance means seeing things as they are, not judging,*
*and being open to receive them."*
Nomi Sharron: Paths to Spiritual Awakening

# The Twenty-Second Blessing

*I am blessed with a sense of humour -*
*- thank you for helping me to call on this frequently, lest I take myself, or others,*
*too seriously*

In "Lonely Hearts" columns [so prevalent in cultures where so many people feel isolated, alienated and lonely] individuals from all walks of life seem to be searching for a partner with a Good Sense Of Humour. Why is this? Why do people looking for a relationship value a sense of humour above intelligence, compassion or love? A sense of humour is a safety valve; it can pave over the cracks in a relationship, help to diffuse difficult situations, avoid confrontations, relieve stress and tension, and keep us from getting sucked into the dramas we create. Humour can bring lightness, laughter and fun into our lives. It can also help us to be more accepting of others, and of the frailties, foibles and 'flaws' that seem to make up the human condition.

A good sense of humour is indeed an important Blessing! It can help us to deflate [a lingering?] judgementalness, when we, or others, don't live up to the high standards we may demand. In personal relationships, a sense of humour is a wonderful tool for diffusing another person's defensiveness and allowing us to move towards mutual recognition and acceptance. And it is a marvellous instrument for pricking inflated dignity, pomposity or self-importance – someone else's, or our own! A good sense of humour helps us not to take ourselves too seriously, and to laugh at our foibles. It can liberate us from remaining stuck in situations that we see only one way. You cannot be a victim when you laugh at yourself! The spiritual path is profound, demanding, and yes, serious; but it is not earnest. We need to remember that the world was created as part of the Divine comedy!

So, lighten up. Let go of solemnity, earnestness, a long face and a heavy heart. Give all your efforts and endeavours their true measure, but don't take yourself too seriously. Use your sense of humour to dispel any negativity, anger or judgementalness in those around you, and to lighten your own dark moods. Recognize and laugh gently at the machinations of your mind and the determined manipulations of your ego. Be inclusive of others, and share your humour with them. Hold yourself lightly; lightness is part of enlightenment. Open up to the gentle incongruities of life, surprise yourself with humour, live in abundant joy. And laugh!

*"Men will confess to treason,*
*murder, arson, false teeth, or a wig.*
*How many of them will own up to a lack of humour?"*
Frank Colby: Essays – 1


*"A well-developed sense of humour*
*is the pole that adds balance to your steps*
*as you walk the tightrope of life."*
William Arthur Ward, writer, most quoted for his "inspirational maxims"


*"A little perspective, like a little humour, goes a long way."*
Allen Klein, businessman, music publisher


*"A day without laughter is a day wasted."*
Charlie Chaplin


*"At the height of laughter,*
*the universe is flung into a kaleidoscope of new possibilities."*
Jean Houston [quoted in The Artist's Way by Julia Cameron]

# The Twenty-Third Blessing

*I am blessed with integrity -*
*- thank you for helping me to manifest this Blessing in all that I am, all that I do*

Living with integrity is fundamental to our spiritual growth. This means being guided at all times by our Higher Self, not by our ego; by the intention always to act out of consideration and compassion, rather than out of self-centred desire. It demands that we consider the best interest of everyone involved in a situation, not just what we might wish for ourselves. This does not mean that we shouldn't get our own needs met; not at all. But we need to do this in a responsible way; not allowing ourselves to be a victim, but not at anyone else's expense either. And we need to act with integrity, whether our actions are witnessed or not. Following the Four Agreements is a portal into behaving with integrity [see quotation below].

Our spiritual journey is a quest to find the voice of our integrity, and listen to it; to [re] connect to our authenticity and autonomy, and manifest the truth of who we are, of what we are. Our integrity is always there to guide us, when we are ready to hear it calling. As our understanding increases that we are all connected and there is no separation, our integrity becomes the lodestar of our life. It expands our awareness, empowers us to be resolute in our commitment to right thought and right action, and brings us closer to the revelations of the All That Is.

Listen to the voice of your integrity, and live according to its directives. Do not be swayed by popular opinion, or live by societal norms that you know to be wrong. Question all certainties, assumptions and beliefs: yours, other people's, and 'society's'. Don't allow yourself to swing on the end of anyone else's yoyo string. Stand up for what you believe, and do what you know to be right. Take responsibility for your actions and honour your commitments. Be strong in your conviction, gentle in your behaviour. Walk your talk – and talk your walk: be an example to others. Manifest your integrity in everything you do and show what is possible, helping to raise the energetic vibrations of the world. Be the best that you are, that you are meant to be. That you have become.

*"Be impeccable with your word;*
*Don't take anything personally;*
*Don't make assumptions;*
*Always do your best."*
Miguel Ruiz: The Four Agreements: A Practical Guide to Personal Freedom


*"What is left when honour is lost?"*
Publilius Syrus: Maxim 265 [first century BCE]


*"This above all: to thine own self be true*
*And it must follow, as the night the day,*
*Thou canst not then be false to any man."*
William Shakespeare: Hamlet, Act 1, scene 3


*"Integrity is doing the right thing,*
*even when no-one is watching."*
C. S. Lewis, novelist, broadcaster, lay theologian


*"Integrity means living and acting in alignment with spiritual law*
*and with our highest vision...*
*inspiring others not with words, but by our example."*
Dan Millman: The Laws of Spirit


*"Do not steal, not even a glance."*
South American Shamanic teaching

# The Twenty-Fourth Blessing

*I am blessed with courage -*
*- thank you for helping me to dare to take risks, and to welcome the unknown*
*without fear*

Our courage is born of our integrity and our growing awareness. We do not need to be 'heroes' to act courageously. Courage may be shown in great deeds that are praised by others, or in small ways, unseen, and unsung. We can show courage by dissenting from the group and standing up for what we know to be right, regardless of how others may behave; and by speaking up for those who are wrongly accused, bullied or threatened, even if it makes us unpopular. Our courage grows with our integrity, to walk our path ethically and bravely. To speak our truth and walk our talk, and act courageously, even when there is no-one to witness it.

Before we can truly act with courage, we need to understand what prevents us. And what prevents us is fear. Behind everything that holds us back lies fear, however deeply it is buried. Fear comes in many guises; until we are 'awake', it will continue to dominate our ego, and our lives. [We shall come back to this again – and again!] There is fear of moving out of our comfort zone, fear of not being good enough, fear of being 'different' or looking foolish; fears embedded in beliefs that lock us into the past or project us with anxiety into the future. Our greatest fear is fear of the unknown. We are fearful of what we might lose if we embrace change, of people to whom we are close abandoning us. But being courageous doesn't mean having no fear; we all have fears. It means recognizing our fears, and having the courage to work through them. It also means showing ourselves to be vulnerable; this is a strength, not a weakness. When we truly connect to our vulnerability, we will recognize it as a Blessing.

Be strong and of good courage as you journey forward. Face your tigers! They have much to teach you. Venture into the unknown without fear. Be ready to jump without a safety net to catch you if you fall. Remind yourself that change opens us up to the fullness of life. Allow the exciting adventure that is your life to unfold in its own unique way, no holds barred. Welcome it fearlessly. Speak your truth, and stand behind your words and your deeds. Fight against injustice, conflict, discord; views that are divisive and sow separation. Counter wrong-doing by showing unconditional love. Let your courage shine as an example to the world.

*"It is not because things are difficult that we do not dare;*
*It is because we do not dare that things are difficult."*
Seneca


*"The price of inaction is far greater than the cost of making a mistake."*
Meister Eckhart, 13th century theologian and mystic


*"I have learned that courage is not the absence of fear,*
*but the triumph over it."*
Nelson Mandela


*"Whatever you dream of doing, begin it.*
*Boldness has genius, magic, and power in it."*
Johann Wolfgang von Goethe


*"No pessimist ever discovered the secret of the stars,*
*or sailed an uncharted land,*
*or opened a new doorway for the human spirit."*
Helen Keller [blind and deaf from birth]


*[Courage is]*
*"to arrive at that place where unbearable truth*
*is preferable to comfortable fiction."*
Nomi Sharron: Then Let the Barrier Fall

# The Twenty-Fifth Blessing

*I am blessed with aspiration -*
*- thank you for helping me to manifest this with integrity, compassion and ruth*

Aspiration is not the same as ambition, and they should not be confused. Aspiration comes from the Higher Self; ambition is an expression of the ego. In our awakening spirituality, we may disdain aspiration along with ambition, and aspire to 'rise above' it. But this is a false degradation of aspiration. The task of our soul is to recognize the collusions of the physical world, and guide our journey through them. The question to ask ourselves is not *what* we do, but *how* we do it; what is our intention behind it. Manifesting our aspirations is part of our human journey, and is to be treasured. What is *not* part of our journey is chasing the fulfilment of ambition, which is rooted in our ego, believing this to be all-important, no matter what the cost. The world is large. There is room for everyone to follow their aspirations; there is no room for the exploitation of others.

We are here in this life to follow our dreams and fulfil our potential – all our potential. When we connect to the *process* of our journey rather than the result, our aspirations are blessed and thrive. They may be large visions of changing the world, bringing peace to war-torn regions or saving the rain forests; or small endeavours within our own community. We may aspire to find a medical or scientific breakthrough, win a Nobel Prize, or raise a family on a farm. Our aspirations may take years to come to fruition, or simply be part of the way we live. Elephants and ants are both part of our world. All our aspirations are of value if they are born in our heart and expressed with integrity and ruth.

Always do your best, whatever you undertake; this is a spiritual imperative! Strive for excellence in all your endeavours, large or small, not in order to gain glory in the world, but because this is the right thing to do. Allow your aspirations to pave your spiritual path, and your spirituality to inform your aspirations. Attempt to reach beyond the horizon, letting your aspirations bring benefit and Blessing to you and to the world. If setting out to swim across the ocean seems daunting, set out with the intention of feeling the waves buoying up your body, the sun on your face. Allow yourself to enjoy the process, experiencing fully each moment. The journey is the goal. And who knows, you may even reach the other side of the ocean!

*"Far away, there in the sunshine,*
*are my highest aspirations.*
*I may not reach them,*
*but I can look up and see their beauty,*
*and try to follow where they lead."*
Louisa May Alcott, novelist, most famous for Little Women


*"Reach high, for stars lie hidden in your soul.*
*Dream deep, for every dream precedes the goal."*
Pamela Vaull Starr, poet and artist


*"It's amazing what you can accomplish*
*when you don't care who gets the credit."*
Harry Truman


*"Start by doing what is necessary; then do what is possible;*
*and suddenly you are doing the impossible."*
Francis of Assisi


*"If I am not for myself, who is for me?*
*And if I am only for myself, what am I?*
*And if not now, when?*
The Mishna: Rabbi Hillel, Avot, chapter 1, verse 14

# The Twenty-Sixth Blessing

*I am blessed with mindfulness and awareness -*
*- thank you for helping me to bring this Blessing into each present moment*

Some of us seem to sleepwalk through our lives, simply allowing life to happen to us, not really living it at all. If we are hungry and eat a meal without awareness, we may be full at the end of it, but we will not feel satisfied. So is it with our lives. If we live without mindfulness, we may continually feel hungry and dissatisfied, because we are not *experiencing* our life. We may wake up one day when we are sixty or seventy years old and wonder where our life has gone. We have not lived it. Living with mindfulness is living in the moment, being fully present to what is around us; being grounded in our body, connected to our heart, and in stillness in our mind. It means seeing things as they are, and not as we may wish them to be. Everything in life has something to teach us.

Buddha talks of mindfulness as the practice of focused attention in each moment. A helpful way to bring mindfulness into your life is to name aloud each action as you perform it. You might say, "Now I am getting dressed…" "Now I am preparing my breakfast…" As your mind wanders, as it will, bring your attention back into your action. Do whatever you are doing *for the sake of doing it,* with full awareness, not thinking about something else. If you are washing the floor, *wash the floor.* How you wash the floor may seem like a trivial matter. But spirituality is actually *about* the way you wash the floor, just as it is about the way you do everything in life. Whether you are washing the floor or meditating, *how* you perform each action is a measure of your spiritual evolvement.

Embracing mindfulness in everything you do is both an expression, and a tool, of your spiritual evolvement. Bring mindfulness into your feelings, your thoughts, your actions. Be awake, aware and alert, and experience each moment fully. Be open to receive whatever the universe offers you. Breathe into the stillness within, into your spiritual heart, and let your mindfulness connect you more profoundly to your Higher Self, and to the Source. Open up to the natural rhythms of the universe, and experience your life more deeply, more meaningfully, more calmly, and more joyously. Be aware of the feelings of others, and the needs of the planet. Be mindful of how you serve.

*"When mindfulness shines its light upon our activity,*
*we recover ourselves*
*and encounter life in the present moment,"*
Thich Nhat Hanh: The Miracle of Mindfulness


*"You become a witness to your own being.*
*You start watching your thoughts, desires, dreams, motives...*
*You create a new kind of awareness within you."*
Osho: The Book of Wisdom


*"Meditation is the dissolution of thoughts in Eternal awareness...*
*knowing without thinking, merging finitude in infinity".*
Voltaire


*"It doesn't matter how far or how fast we move forward.*
*What matters is how much of ourselves we take along on our journey."*
Oriah Mountain Dreamer: The Invitation


*"Life is a dance.*
*Mindfulness is witnessing that dance."*
Amit Ray: Mindfulness: Living in the Moment, Living in the Breath.

# The Twenty-Seventh Blessing

*I am blessed with intention*
*- thank you for helping me to focus my intention on the highest good of myself*
*and others*

Intention is the expression of our Higher Self, the awareness that all benefit to our own life is inextricably bound up with the good of others. We may find that we have been acting out of will, that is, personal ego desire to do things for our own benefit. But intention is profoundly different from will. Intention comes from a place of mindfulness, to flow with the natural movement of life, driven by the wish to act for the highest good of all. The Blessing of intention reminds us that we are all interconnected, part of each other, part of the same Oneness. By harming another being, we are actually harming ourselves. Living with intention leads us to right relationship with ourselves, with others, and with the universe.

Intention is a direction, a process. It is the manifestation of our awareness in action, the expression of our highest integrity. It empowers the way we walk our path; it is the gateway to experiential knowing and wisdom. The more we act with intention, the less possible it becomes for us to act out of ego desire. By living with intention, we honour our deepest self, we nourish our spirit, and simultaneously bring benefit to the world around us. Intention fuels our clarity of purpose, and helps us to see things as they really are, not to 'fudge'. Our journey becomes more focused, more resolute, unencumbered by clutter and confusion. Our intention grows stronger with its practice, and expands our awareness and compassion.

Intention paves the path of our spirituality, and is also its manifestation; the purpose and the way of realising it. Let intention infuse your thoughts and your actions. Let it expand your courage, your compassion, and your trust, and look for these qualities in others; it is spiritual lore that like attracts like. And of course do no harm. If everyone lived by this dictum alone, there would be no more wars, no violence, no greed, no exploitation; a world at peace with itself. Use your intention to be an example to others. The more you act for the highest good of all, the more you attract the good to yourself, and to others. Act always from your heart, the home of your pure intention, your sacred centre. Open yourself up with intention to the love and joy and abundance of Blessings that the universe offers you. Feel your life enriched beyond measure.

*"If you change the way you look at things,*
*the things you look at change."*
Wayne Dyer, writer and motivational speaker


*"Intentional living means making choices for your life*
*based on your highest integrity."*
Source Unknown


*"A gift consists not in what is done or given,*
*but in the intention of the giver or doer."*
Seneca: Moral Essays, Volume lll – de Beneficiis


*"All great acts are ruled by intention.*
*What you mean is what you get."*
Brenna Yovanoff: The Replacement


*"How can I win if you lose?"*
Old Shamanic saying


*"Intention is the expression of our Higher Self,*
*the manifestation of consciousness in action."*
Nomi Sharron: Tony Samara, A Modern Shaman… and Beyond

# The Twenty-Eighth Blessing

*I am blessed with happiness –*
*  - thank you for helping me to know that all happiness comes from within*

It is a spiritual truth that happiness can only come from within. [Please read this sentence again. Accepting its truth can transform your life.] Happiness cannot be found in the external world. What we find in the outside world is an illusion of happiness: fleeting and ephemeral, it evaporates when its 'cause' disappears. The root of our unhappiness is our separation from the Source and from the Divine within us. So we create a 'need' for things that we think will make us happy: money, approval, power. This 'need' comes from limited beliefs. If we are looking for happiness in the outside world, we need to change our beliefs. We search for happiness outside ourselves when we are unhappy – and we are unhappy precisely *because* we are searching for happiness outside. We need to get off this treadmill and begin to look within.

We often look for happiness in other people, and particularly in one 'special' person. But nobody can 'make you' happy; nor indeed angry, jealous, resentful, or anything else. They may trigger these feelings in you, but your feelings are yours and come from within you. Own them. It is *your choice* what you feel. In a loving relationship, your partner gives you the opportunity to manifest the joy that is already within you, and reflects this back to you. *But everything you need to live a joyous life is already inside you.* Everything. So stop looking for happiness in the approval of other people, or in the acquisition of more material goods. Take responsibility for your happiness. Don't expect anyone else to provide it [nobody else can] or blame others for what you lack. Your happiness is already within you!

Recognizing your happiness within is the fulfilment of your soul's yearning for harmony. So let go of your ego games; your happiness does not live there. Take off the masks that cloud your joy; they are tools of the ego, to keep you in its power. Reconnect to your spiritual essence, your Higher Self, and let this guide you inwards, to the source of your happiness. Remind yourself – again and again – that everything you need for a joyous life is within you. When you really take this on board, you transform your life. Manifest this joy in the present moment – in each present moment – and allow the light of your delight to shine forth and illuminate the path.

*"If you learn only one thing in this lifetime, let it be this:*
*you are responsible for creating your own happiness."*
Bartholomew [Channelled Source]


*"Happiness cannot be travelled to, owned, earned or worn.*
*It is the spiritual experience of living every minute*
*with love, grace and gratitude."*
Denis Waitley, writer and motivational speaker


*"The basic condition for being happy*
*is our consciousness of being happy."*
Thich Nhat Hanh: Peace in Every Step


*"Happiness is not having what you want.*
*It is wanting what you have."*
Original Source Unknown


*"Be happy for this moment.*
*For this moment is your life."*
Omar Khayyam


*"The light that belongs to you is the light of joy."*
A Course in Miracles [Channelled Source]

# The Twenty-Ninth Blessing

*I am blessed with abundance -*
*- thank you for helping me to recognize my abundance in all things*

Abundance is everywhere. The universe showers infinite abundance on all who are open to receive it – spiritual riches, as well as the gifts of Mother Earth, and material well-being. Welcoming this Blessing, we connect to the abundance of the All That Is, and are embraced and enriched by it. Abundance is not so much about what we have, as about what we feel, and how we live. It is an attitude of mind, of heart. It encourages us to live in a generosity of spirit, letting go of our ego-driven desires as we merge into the expansiveness of the Source. The more we tune in to the limitless flow of abundance in the universe, the more we create 'abundance consciousness', and the more we attract abundance to ourselves. Living with abundance consciousness changes the way we are.

Abundance consciousness is a state of grace that is fed when we manifest our Blessing of gratitude. It cannot include envy, judgementalness, self-righteousness, blame or guilt; nor anything that is divisive or mean-spirited. We may believe that life is a struggle, that suffering and hardship are inevitable, that we will always be poor. We may feel that we don't deserve any better. Or that material wealth is incompatible with spiritual living. [It is not, if you come by it ethically, and share it with others.] This comes from a 'poverty consciousness'. And our beliefs about everything are self-fulfilling. If you believe that you don't deserve, you will not receive. What you believe, what you invite into your life, is *your choice.* So start the process of letting go of suffering and struggle, and make space to welcome the Blessings that the universe showers upon you.

Open your heart to abundance, embrace the recognition that life is joyous, empowering, and infinitely enriching. Choose to live in abundance consciousness, and see how abundance manifests more and more in your life. Spread abundance consciousness among others, give, and be open to receive. Remind yourself that no-one's abundance diminishes anyone else's. Show gratitude for spiritual riches and for material well-being. Enjoy the abundance that Mother Earth showers on you, and give something back by supporting her with your love and care. Manifest a generosity of spirit in everything you do. Delight, share and celebrate!

*"Life in abundance comes only through great love."*
Elbert Hubbard


*"Who is rich? He who is satisfied with his lot."*
The Talmud: Ethics of the Fathers, chapter 4, verse 1


*"Abundance is being open to receive."*
Many people have been credited with this quotation


*"Abundance is not something we acquire.*
*It is something we tune into."*
Wayne Dyer


*"From the Light of God that we are.*
*From the Love of God that we are.*
*From the Power of God that we are.*
*From the Heart of God that we are.*
*We dwell in the midst of Abundance.*
*The Abundance of God is our infinite Source."*
From The Abundance Prayer

# The Thirtieth Blessing

*I am blessed with generosity –*
*– thank you for helping me to be generous to myself and others*

Generosity flows from abundance consciousness. It comes from our heart, a manifestation of our spiritual awareness. It is not connected to how affluent we are materially: rich people may be mean spirited, poor people hugely generous. Generosity is about who we are, and the way we live. It is not about giving away, but about sharing: our time, compassion, energy, friendship, our love. Being generous is also about sharing money and material possessions. If you have difficulty giving money, ask yourself what money symbolizes for you – status, control, power, being envied by others? It is these things you are finding it difficult to part with. The more you are able to let go of your attachment to money, the easier it becomes to live in a spirit of generosity. And the more you share, the more enriched you become.

The Blessing of generosity is about who we are, as well as what we do. When we are connected to the abundance of the All That Is, expressing gratitude for its myriad Blessings, how can we not act generously? This means giving to ourselves, nurturing and loving ourselves – and occasionally spoiling ourselves! – as well as sharing what we have with others. As we nurture ourselves, we open ourselves up to act generously with others. This does not mean giving *to* others in a way that can diminish them, as though they are needy and therefore less worthy than we; but rather sharing *with* others, a transaction among equals. Giving in this spirit is a joy to those who receive, and to those who give. The more you allow yourself to feel the joy of giving, the more your joy will increase.

Manifest your abundance consciousness, and the knowledge that there is plenty for everyone. The more you live in this spirit, the more generously you share, the more abundance flows to you. We are told in the Bible that those who owned fields were obligated to allow poor people to glean around the edges. And all but the very poorest were enjoined to give tithes [a tenth of what they earned]. You might like to follow this example, and give ten per cent of what you earn to charity. Spread abundance consciousness by the way you live and give. Celebrate, and be an example to others. Allow your generosity to radiate out into the world. Be generous in sharing yourself, your possessions, your love – all your Blessings – with others. And be blessed and enriched sevenfold.

*"When you give yourself, you receive more than you give."*
Antoine de Saint-Exupery, poet and writer, most famously of The Little Prince


*"Giving is essential for spiritual unfoldment,*
*for until we give abundantly,*
*we don't realize that we are not the giver;*
*we are just a channel for giving."*
Satguru Sivaya Subramuniyaswami: Gurudeva Weekly Calendar


*"No-one has ever become poor by giving."*
Anne Frank: The Diary of Anne Frank


*"The Meaning of life is to find your gift.*
*The Purpose of life is to give it away."*
Pablo Picasso


*"All you have shall some day be given.*
*Therefore give now,*
*that the season of giving may be yours and not your inheritors."*
Kahlil Gibran: The Prophet

# The Thirty-First Blessing

*I am blessed with compassion -*
*- thank you for helping me to be compassionate towards myself and all sentient beings*

Compassion is the beating heart of spirituality: compassion for ourselves, for others, for all sentient beings. First, we need to give compassion to ourselves; only then are we able to give it to others. Compassion is born in the meeting place of our spirituality and our humanity. It dissolves our judgementalness, our guilt, our sense of shame, and helps us to confront our fears, and transcend our ego games. Often, we blame ourselves for our mistakes. But 'mistakes', as we know, are simply a tool for learning. We need to learn their lessons, and then allow compassion to heal us. Compassion is the bridge between accepting ourselves, as we are, with all our perceived flaws, fears, and failures, and living our lives with discernment and integrity. Compassion for ourselves expands as we walk this bridge, transforming the way we see ourselves, and so the way we live.

Recognizing the essential humanness of others, accepting them as they are, we can reach out to them from our compassion. For others act out of their fears and frustrations, their pain and disappointments, their sense of inadequacy or unworthiness, just as we do. Understanding this can help us to be compassionate towards others, and so reaffirm the humanity at the heart of their being. And anyone whom we feel has wronged or hurt us may best teach us the value of compassion; as we open up to spiritual awareness, we may also show them compassion. True compassion grows from connecting to our heart and our Higher Self. It blesses and sustains us, and others. It makes us whole.

Give yourself permission to be compassionate with yourself, to nurture yourself lovingly and gently, to accept yourself as you are. [Yes, we shall repeat this many times! It is a basic tenet of the spiritual path to accept ourselves, and give ourselves love and compassion.] Inhabit this Blessing, and share it with others: those who have a long-standing place in your life, and those who touch you but fleetingly. Compassion expands as we bestow it upon others – for them and for us. Use your compassion also to care for Mother Earth, and listen to her needs. Treat all creatures, all of nature, with gentleness and compassion. Growing compassion is an expression of your deep connection to the Divine, within you and all around you. Allow it to expand your heart. This is a profound marker on your spiritual journey.

*"If your compassion does not include yourself, it is incomplete."*
Buddha


*"Compassion is the quality that sees the inner needs*
*behinds its expression.*
*It looks behind anger and sees the sadness,*
*behind coldness to the fear."*
Brahma Kumaris: Pocket Book of Wisdom


*"Until he extends his circle of compassion to include all living things,*
*man will not himself find peace."*
Albert Schweitzer


*"Compassion is the basis of all morality."*
Arthur Schopenhauer


*"Within all beings there is the seed of perfection.*
*But compassion is required in order to activate that seed,*
*which is inherent in our hearts..."*
The Dalai Lama: The Art of Happiness

# The Thirty-Second Blessing

*I am blessed with the knowledge that I create my own reality –*
*- thank you for helping me to create the reality envisioned by my Higher Self*

The physical reality that we experience is created by our perception. We each experience reality in our own way, dictated by our beliefs, and coloured by our emotions, assumptions, expectations, and indeed, our fears. But we also *create* our own reality; this is a spiritual truth. [Another sentence to read again, accept its truth, and begin to transform your life!] We not only create our experience of reality, we also *create our own reality.* Change on the outside only comes about through change on the inside first. Knowing this defines who we are. The outer world is a mirror of our inner world, reflecting back to us whatever we project. Our ego mind, or our Higher Self, ensures that the reality we manifest affirms either our rigid beliefs, or our deepest yearnings. Either way, they are always self-fulfilling prophecies.

Accepting the truth that you create your own reality means taking responsibility for your life. Honouring this truth can transform your life. But now there is no-one else to blame! The reality that you manifest reflects the changes you are creating: whoever and whatever crosses your path, you have in some way 'invited' into your reality. It happens for a reason; nothing is random. Each has something to give you. Something to teach you. So be open to receive. Make a leap of faith! Consciousness creates reality, reality does not create consciousness. [Even quantum physics has finally accepted this!] Recognizing this offers you a portal into a deeper spiritual knowing, connecting you more directly to the world of physical reality, and more profoundly to the limitless worlds beyond.

The reality that you create is born of your consciousness. Be mindful in the creating. Let go of what limits you, what makes you fearful. Create the reality envisioned by your Higher Self, a reality that will bring into your life people and situations that enrich and sustain you, that bring you balance, meaning and gratitude. Like attracts like. Invite into your life people who affirm your integrity and courage, your openness and compassion, your joy in being fully alive in the moment. Hold up a mirror to a world that reflects harmony, peace, caring and sharing, and bathe in its glory. Connect to the Oneness of the All That Is, and receive the abundant Blessings that are showered upon you. Manifest them in the reality you create. A reality that smiles back to you with love.

*"Be the change you want to see in the world."*
Mahatma Ghandi


*"This place is a dream.*
*Only a sleeper considers it real."*
Jelaluddin Rumi


*"Two men looked out through prison bars;*
*one saw mud, the other saw stars."*
Source Unknown


*"Don't wait for extraordinary opportunities.*
*Seize common occasions and make them great."*
Orison Swett Marden, writer of inspirational books


*"Like attracts like.*
*Whatever the conscious mind thinks and believes,*
*the subconscious creates."*
Brian Adams: How to Succeed


*"Two friends visit a foreign city together.*
*One sees an exciting place,*
*with warm friendly people,*
*interesting historical architecture,*
*and exotic restaurants serving delicious local dishes.*
*The other sees a fearful place,*
*full of threatening and hostile people,*
*dirty old buildings and food not fit for the dog.*
*Same city, same sites; two different realities."*
Nomi Sharron: Paths to Spiritual Awakening

# The Thirty-Third Blessing

*I am blessed with living in the present moment -*
*- thank you for helping me to know that this is <u>the only place</u> we can live*

Living in the present moment is all there is. We can only ever live in the present, this moment, now. When we truly embrace this, our lives are transformed. The present moment is all there is. Everything else is illusion. The past is a country we have left behind; what lingers are memories, or myths that we tell ourselves, about what happened, or didn't happen. The future is a fantasy kingdom we can visit only in our imagination. But the only place we can ever *live* is the present moment. If we squander it, it will not return. Everything else is memory – true or false – or projection. Time is an illusion created by our ego mind to prevent us from being present, in the present, and so keep us under its control.

Living in the present moment is all there is. Only in the present moment can you be grounded in the stillness of your heart, in mindfulness, connected to the sacred within you, and all around you. Only in the present moment are you able to receive the Blessings that the universe is offering you. Only in the present moment can life truly be lived. Accepting the truth of this brings a shift in perception, in consciousness. Being truly present in the present moment creates a different energy field around you, a higher vibration. When you let go of the illusion of time, the present moment expands to fill the space and open a portal to the infinite now.

Celebrate your life – Now! In this moment. Breathe. Be present to yourself: to your breathing, your feelings, your intuition, your intention in this moment. Be present to the world around you, to your connection to the All That Is. Let go of the busyness of your mind, and embrace the freedom of this moment, fully alive and awake. This moment holds all of life. In this moment, be who you really are; fully inhabit your intuition, your integrity, your wholeness. Re-awaken the life of your heart and your soul; rediscover in this moment their energy, their compassion, their wisdom. Be open to receive the abundance of the universe. Remind yourself that you can only ever live in the present moment, in the Now. Whether you do this consciously, or not, is the difference that defines your life.

*"Make the Now the primary focus of your life...*
*Whatever the present moment contains, accept it...*
*This will miraculously transform your whole life."*
Eckhart Tolle: The Power of Now.


*"Past and future veil God from our sight;*
*burn up both of them with fire."*
Jalaluddin Rumi


*"How wonderful it is that nobody need wait a single moment*
*before starting to improve the world."*
Anne Frank: The Diary of Anne Frank


*"I avoid looking forward or backward,*
*and try to keep looking upward."*
Charlotte Bronte


*"Be happy in the moment. That's enough.*
*Each present moment is all we need, not more."*
Mother Teresa


*"Look to this day, for it is life;*
*The very life of life...*
*For yesterday is but a memory,*
*And tomorrow is only a vision...*
*Look well, therefore, to this day."*
Sanskrit Hymn

# The Thirty-Fourth Blessing

*I am blessed with detachment –*
*– thank you for helping me to let go of all attachment, all attachment*

The Blessing of detachment is transformative, but it is often misunderstood. It does *not* mean being uninvolved with life; not at all. It means being deeply engaged with life, but at the same time stepping back and observing our actions. Attachment is a form of slavery, and most of us are enslaved to something: to our beliefs, our assumptions, our certainties; to our ego self that sees itself as separate, competitive, judgemental, relentless in its search for gratification and approval. Detachment means not having an agenda, doing things for their own sake, without attachment to outcome. Being a witness to our life. Embracing the Blessing of detachment marks a great step forward on our spiritual journey. It is far more than 'letting go', which is 'allowing'. Detachment is an active choice, a portal to a new way of being. It is indeed transformational.

We all need to detach ourselves from emotional bondage. This means, once we are adult, relinquishing emotional dependence on our parents. Our identity, the structure of our ego, our view of the world and our place within it, will all have been coloured by our parents, even if not consciously; we hold onto an extension of their 'baggage'. We need to detach from this emotional enmeshment. We also need to relinquish emotional dependence in an intimate relationship; to stop seeing the other as an object of desire, whose function is to fill the lack in our lives. We have to detach from *neediness:* of anyone else's time, energy, attention, approval, friendship, or love, in order to feel good about ourselves. Remember, all happiness is within us; we choose our own feelings, and no-one else has the power to make us feel anything.

Step back and observe yourself. Watch your feelings, the machinations of your mind, your actions. Don't get caught up in the dramas created by your ego, or your desire to control life. You can't! Don't take anything personally, don't take offence, and don't get caught up in other people's agendas for you. This is their stuff, not yours. Try to be equally unmoved by praise or blame. This is a shift of gear on your spiritual journey. Be a witness to your life, and witness the witness. Inhabit the Blessing of detachment and connect to your autonomy, your integrity, your wholeness. Live in detachment and let it transform and liberate your life.

*"You have a right to perform actions,*
*but you are not entitled to the fruits of action.*
*Never consider yourself to be the cause of the results of your activities,*
*and never be attached to the outcome."*
Bhaghavad Gita, chapter 2


*"True detachment isn't a separation from life,*
*but the absolute freedom ... to explore living."*
Ron W. Rathbun: The Mind and Self-Reflection


*"Five young men were passing through a village*
*carrying a heavy boat on their heads.*
*'Why are you carrying a boat on your heads?' asked the villagers.*
*'The boat brought us across the river*
*and saved us from the wild animals on the other side.*
*It saved our lives. We will carry it on our heads forever.'*
*There comes a time when we need to thank the boat for its help,*
*and then let it go."*
Buddha


*"Attachment is the great fabricator of illusions;*
*reality can be attained only by someone who is detached."*
Simone Weil, French philosopher, mystic and writer

# The Thirty-Fifth Blessing

*I am blessed with balance -*
*- thank you for helping me to be guided by the rhythms and harmony of the universe*

The world came into being through balance. Balance is created by the ebb and flow of the seeming polarities of the universe that exist within everything: day and night, heat and cold, masculine and feminine. These are not two opposing forces, nor are they the two ends of a line, for nothing is linear. All 'opposites' are actually two aspects of a union, forever feeding into each other, pulling away and reconverging. Neither can exist without its contra-force. For how could we know a mountain without a valley, sunrise without sunset, fullness without hunger? Without balance, the universe as we know it could not exist.

Receiving this Blessing helps us to tune in to the rhythms of the universe and create greater balance within ourselves: balance between head and heart, the physical and the spiritual, work and play, activity and stillness. Balance between taking care of our survival needs and looking after our bodies, and time devoted to creative pursuits and feeding our soul. Balance between time alone with ourselves, and time spent doing things with, and for, others. And of course they are all part of the same Oneness. At the moment, masculine and feminine energies are out of balance in the world; we all need to connect more deeply with Divine feminine energy – especially if we are male – thus helping to heal ourselves and bring healing to the world. Balance is simultaneously holding within our consciousness the seeming dualities of spiritual paradox; and at the same time recognizing the non-duality of the All That Is.

Embrace this Blessing and bring greater balance into your life. Observe where you put your energy. Give attention to those areas of your life that are getting too little, so that each has its true measure. If you feel that something in your life is out of kilter, still your mind and focus on your breath, breathing deeply and rhythmically, in harmony with the primal rhythms of the universe. Open yourself up to live each moment within the rhythms of nature, connected to the Source. Let the highest vibrations of the cosmos guide you to live in your still centre. Receive the Blessings that this brings: healing, wholeness, serenity; a profound knowing that all is as it is meant to be in your life. That all is well. Live in harmony with yourself, with others, and with the world around you. Feel the deep joy and peace that this brings.

*"To every thing there is a season,*
*and a time to every purpose under the heavens..."*
The Old Testament: Ecclesiastes 3, verse 1


*"So divinely is the world organized that every one of us,*
*in our place and time,*
*is in balance with everything else."*
Johann Wolfgang von Goethe


*"If gravity is the glue that holds the universe together,*
*balance is the key that unlocks it's secrets."*
Dan Millman: The Laws of Spirit


*"Balance is the perfect state of still water.*
*Let that be our model."*
Confucius


*"The longest journey is the journey from the head to the heart.*
*When balance guides our steps,*
*we understand that how we journey is the way..."*
Nomi Sharron: Paths to Spiritual Awakening

# The Thirty-Sixth Blessing

*I am blessed with intuition and insight -*
*- thank you for helping me to recognize this voice of the Divine within me*

Our intuition and insight is the voice of our soul awakening us to truths we know but may have forgotten. Its role in our life is often misunderstood: it is not a seer predicting the future, but rather a guide to help us live in the present moment. Our intuition has different ways of speaking to us. As we become more used to connecting to it, we will more easily recognize its different manifestations. We may hear our intuition as a voice inside our head. Or we may feel it as a stirring in our heart. Or we may visualize it as a personified being, an angel or spirit guide. [One of the ways that our spirit guides speak to us is through our intuition.] It doesn't matter how we envisage our intuition, only that we listen to it. And trust its wisdom.

The voice of our intuition gives expression to our insight. Our head is limited to giving us factual information; our intuition can guide us to reveal a knowing beyond. It is the bridge that links the physical world with the Source. Our intuition is the revelation of our soul on its human journey, the gift that it brings with it to inform, and give meaning to, our life on this earth. Through the voice of our intuition come insight and inspiration. It infuses our spontaneity, our creativity, and our imagination. Our intuition lives in our Higher Self, a manifestation of our highest good. It is a channel for bringing us profound messages. It is the voice of the Divine speaking within us.

Listen to the voice of your intuition, and be guided by its wisdom. Don't dismiss it out of hand, or let your ego mind suppress it. And don't be influenced by the scepticism of others. Acknowledge that it has your highest good at heart. Open yourself up to the insight it offers you, trust it, and act upon it. You will be giving yourself a priceless gift. Or rather, you will have recognized that a priceless gift has been bestowed upon you by grace. Connect to its power and the wisdom that it brings. Acknowledge that by listening to your intuition, you have gained insight enough to see beyond physical 'reality' and accept a deeper truth. Let your insight inform your behaviour, and empower, nourish, and enrich your life.

*"Sell your cleverness and buy bewilderment;*
*Cleverness is mere opinion, bewilderment is intuition."*
Jalaluddin Rumi


*"The best vision is in-sight."*
Malcolm Forbes, entrepreneur and publisher of Forbes Magazine


*"A moment's insight is sometimes worth a life's experience."*
Oliver Wendell Holmes: The Professor at the Breakfast Table


*"We are all walking towards death,*
*but we never know when death will touch us.*
*It is our duty, therefore, to look inside us,*
*to be grateful for each moment."*
Paulo Coelho: Like the Flowing River


*"Follow your inner call, for this moment is yours alone."*
Saint Germain & Ashamarae McNamara: The Blueprint of Oneness


*"If the doors of perception were cleansed,*
*everything would appear to man as it is, infinite."*
William Blake

# The Thirty-Seventh Blessing

*I am blessed with dreams for my life's journey -*
*- thank you for helping me to follow them with imagination, tenacity and courage*

We are here in this life to live our dreams, the dreams that we brought with us into this world, dreamt before we were born; the dreams that are our soul's purpose in this incarnation. They are the guiding light of our journey in this life. They represent the true essence of our being, embodying our quest for truth and understanding. Recognizing them connects us to our Higher Self, to the sacred within. As we follow the dreams held in our soul, the unfolding meaning of our life is revealed. Manifesting our dreams, the yearning of our soul, reaffirms our connection to the Source, to our being in the Oneness of the All That Is. This supports and sustains the questing of our soul.

You are here to live your dreams. There will always be people telling you that your dreams are impossible to fulfil. You have to be 'sensible', build a career, earn a living. Who are you to go off and live some crazy dream, just because you want to? Who are you not to? If you suppress your dreams, you diminish yourself and impoverish your life. Behind whatever you feel is preventing you from following your dreams, it is always fear. When you decide to follow your dreams, the universe supports you. The practicalities get sorted. The obstacles that seemed insurmountable dissolve. You cannot know where your dreams will lead you; all you can do is follow, and watch in gratitude the miraculous way they unfold your life.

Acknowledge that you have dreams. Give yourself permission to dream the dreams you abandoned as a child. Allow yourself to discover, uncover, recover, them. And then verbalize them. This is important; it gives them form, an existence that you can recognize. Remind yourself that this is why you have come here: to live your dreams and expand your courage. Know that you are worthy of manifesting them. Ask the universe for help. As you do, the energy of the All That Is will gather to support you. Then, ask yourself: Are you ready to stand opposite the fear and risk everything to follow your heart? To stand in the centre of the fire, with arms outstretched, and shout "Yes!" to the universe? This is your soul calling to you. Follow its voice with courage. Remember, today's dreams are tomorrow's Blessings. Your highest intention is the magic that fuels your dreams.

*"You are here to live your dreams."*
Sabine Walczuch, visionary, spiritual photographer, artist


*"I have spread my dreams beneath your feet.
Tread softly because you tread on my dreams."*
William Butler Yeats


*"The future belongs to those who believe in the beauty of their dreams."*
Eleanor Roosevelt


*"Walk as if you are kissing the Earth with your feet."*
Thich Nhat Hanh: Peace in Every Step


*"If your dreams don't scare you out of your wits,
they're not big enough!"*
Source Unknown


*"Dreams are the blueprint of the story
that your soul is writing with your life."*
Nomi Sharron: Paths to Spiritual Awakening

# The Thirty-Eighth Blessing

*I am blessed with knowing ritual -*
*   - thank you for helping me to celebrate in ritual more than my mind can grasp*

Ritual is a powerful tool for transformation. It is an outward celebration, marking an inner journey. It connects us to the deep symbolism of our soul. Ritual is a Blessing to celebrate, even if we do not understand its meaning. Performing a ritual is a way of bringing the holy into the mundane and consecrating it. Many hidden things may be revealed through ritual. It is a ceremony of symbolic purification, providing an opportunity for cleansing and healing. Ritual is a place of mystery, an invitation to our spirit guides to bring us knowledge and wisdom from other dimensions. It is a place where the Divine presence manifests most strongly. Ritual is a way of calling back our soul into our body.

Rituals form part of the tradition of most religious and spiritual paths. Ancient rituals incorporate within them the spiritual energy of those who have performed them down the ages, bringing to our own celebration of these rituals added spiritual power. Rituals can also be personal, created by each of us to mark and transform our own life experiences. They provide a safe place for us to let go of unwanted beliefs, and get off the treadmill of our automatic reactions. Performing rituals on a regular basis gives them added power, and helps us to connect more profoundly to the Source. Creating and sharing rituals with others can heal relationships, strengthen bonds of love and friendship, and bring us together in the Oneness of the All That Is.

Celebrate your life with ritual. Follow rituals of a particular tradition, or create your own. Or do both. Ritual may be silent, or it may use words; your own, or quotations that resonate with you. Performing rituals marks a transition, from what was to what is, now. Create rituals to mark particular events in your life, or rites of passage. Be open to receive, and allow grace to inspire your rituals. Establish a special sacred place for your ritual and add to its power. Bring to this place objects that are meaningful to you: crystals, candles, feathers, stones, tree bark, incense, photographs, poems, etc. Honour and enrich your life with ritual. Let it bring you purification and transformation. Through the symbolism of ritual, connect to the Mystery of the Source. Become a channel for Divine energy and healing and love.

*"Ritual is necessary for us to know anything."*
Ken Kesey, American novelist, part of the 1950s counterculture


*"The unique value of the 'authentic' work of art*
*has its basis in ritual."*
Walter Benjamin, German philosopher


*"All ritual is an opportunity for transformation."*
Starhawk, American writer, activist, known as a theorist of feminist Neopaganism


*"In every ancient culture, rituals are performed...*
*as a way of understanding that the energy of the soul is indestructible."*
Marina Abramovic, Serbian performance artist based in New York


*"Ritual allows those who cannot will themselves out of the secular*
*to perform the spiritual,*
*as dancing allows the tongue-tied a ceremony of love."*
Andre Dubus, American short story writer


*"By performing apparently absurd rituals,*
*you get in touch with something deep in your soul,*
*in the oldest part of yourself,*
*the part closest to the origin of everything."*
Paulo Coelho: Aleph

# The Thirty-Ninth Blessing

*I am blessed with healing –*
*  - thank you for helping me to heal myself, and be a channel for healing others*
*and the planet*

Our purpose in this life is to learn to love better and to heal – ourselves, others, and the planet. It is a journey into healing and wholeness. Healing is holistic: it means healing our lives, not just our bodies. Physical sickness or pain are only the symptoms of dis-ease, in our emotions, or our minds; the tip of the iceberg that warns of danger beneath the surface. Of course we may want to alleviate the symptoms of illness and pain. But real healing only begins when we go into our woundedness, and recognize that the causes of physical illness do not lie in our body; when we face the things that are making us sick: suppressed anger, resentment, judgementalness, blame, guilt. And no, this is not a call for a guilt trip! Rather, an opportunity to look within and learn. Whether we are physically ill or not, we all have need of healing.

Physical pain or illness is often the catalyst that propels us onto our healing path. Illness is never random. And it is not something to be fought and vanquished, but rather welcomed for the lessons it has come to teach us; a nudge for us to examine our life and see what is out of kilter. This may be a difficult concept to accept at first. Try to stay with it. For once you accept that illness is a Blessing, and is not just about a sick body, you can start to unravel what it has come to teach you, and begin your healing journey. Healing comes by looking inwards and not running away, by acknowledging and facing our fears, by accepting what is and dealing with it. This is the key to healing, to becoming whole.

Recognize that the healing process is a journey of self discovery. Allow yourself to go deeply into your woundedness, your dark places, your vulnerability. Stay with whatever comes up: images, memories, fragments, emotions, and yes, fears. Let this teach you what you need to learn. Be gentle with yourself. If you are ill, check what was happening in your life when you became ill. What was out of balance. Ask yourself, what are your pay-offs for staying sick. Be brave! This can be the key to your healing. What are you prepared to do to heal? What are you not prepared to do? Your answers may surprise you! Connect to the healing energy of the Source and ask for help. Allow yourself to be a channel for Divine healing: for others, and for Mother Earth. Your healing journey can lead you to wholeness, empowerment, and a greatly enriched life.

*"No medical intervention can heal you*
*until your spirit has begun to make the changes*
*that the illness was designed to inspire."*
Carolyn Myss: Why People Don't Heal and How They Can


*"You already have the precious mixture that will make you well.*
*Use it."*
Jelaluddin Rumi


*"Love is the great miracle cure.*
*Loving ourselves works miracles in our lives."*
Louise L. Hay: You can Heal Your Life


*"Healing does not mean going back to the way things were before,*
*but rather allowing what is now to move us closer to God."*
Ram Dass, American spiritual teacher


*"As I heal myself,*
*I open myself up to become a channel for healing others and the world."*
Nomi Sharron: Paths to Spiritual Awakening

# The Fortieth Blessing

*I am blessed with trust -*

*- thank you for helping me to trust the Divine unfolding of my life*

Trust is the unwavering knowing of the heart, when nothing makes sense to the mind. All spiritual work requires deep trust, a willingness to accept what we do not understand. Trust paves our spiritual path: trusting Divine will, trusting our intuition and the wisdom of our Higher Self, trusting that life will unfold in its own rightful way. Trust is a measure of our spiritual awakening. It is not passive. It is a deliberate choice, both a tool and a result of growing consciousness. When we trust, we connect to the voice of the Divine within us, and the perfection of the All That Is. The Bible tells us that when Moses assembled the Children of Israel in the wilderness to receive the Ten Commandments, they said, "Na'aseh v'nishma" ["we shall do and we shall hear"]. They agreed to do the will of God before they heard what it entailed. Manifesting this trust is transformational.

Open your heart and allow this place of deep trust to be born within you. Let go of your struggle to control life. This comes from a place of fear, when you are out of control! Trust is the opposite of fear. It allows you to let go – of your certainties, your assumptions, your judgementalness, your self-righteousness. Trusting means letting yourself be vulnerable, exposed. This is strength; it is not being gullible or naïve. Don't be afraid to step out of your comfort zone and let go of the familiar. In its place you make space for wisdom, affirmation, truth. Trust the goodness in others, but don't rely on them in a way that disempowers you. Trust is a Blessing for you, and a gift that you offer to life.

Remind yourself that Creation is perfect as it is. Trust your life and allow it to unfold as a manifestation of this perfection. The universe is here to embrace and support you. Trust the unknown. Move into it fearlessly, and with joy. This is the great adventure of your life! Trust that your life is guided, and that knowing, and not knowing, are each a Blessing. Be open to receive what is offered. Have faith in the Divine Source, and in the Divine perfection within you; and, of course, they are the same. Let trust unfold your life as it is meant to be, and guide you to fulfil your purpose on this earth. Through trust, meaning, wisdom and truth are revealed.

*"One does not discover new lands*
*without consenting to lose sight of the shore for a very long time."*
Andre Gide

*"Trust dares the soul to go further than it can see."*
William Clarke, musician

*"Trust in God is the light that guides our way."*
Mother Teresa

*"Faith is not belief without proof,*
*but trust without reservation."*
D. Elton Trueblood, American Quaker author

*"Faith is a bird that before it feels dawn breaking,*
*sings while it is still dark."*
Rabindranath Tagore

*"Trust is the silence of God."*
Simone Weil: Waiting on God

# The Forty-First Blessing

*I am blessed with the awareness of miracles -*
*- thank you for helping me to recognize their presence and invite them into my life*

Miracles cross our path every day. They are manifest in the physical world, but usually we don't see them. We are human and spiritual beings, and we exist simultaneously in many realms. Miracles are a portal to higher dimensions. They are 'supernatural', but only in the way that all our Blessings are, coming from the Divine Source. Miracles happen all around us; they are a natural phenomenon. But we see them only when we are awake. We need to expand our consciousness, to open our eyes, and our hearts, and recognize them. Miracles are revelations of Spirit, showing us truth and teaching us spiritual wisdom. They offer us a shift in perception. We do not have to 'believe in' them, only to acknowledge their presence.

Nothing in life is random. What we may think of as chance synchronicities are actually small miracles. Anything that crosses our path may be a sign of a miracle: a feather falling at our feet, a lighted candle in a stranger's window, a life-changing encounter that has no logical explanation. Miracles are a manifestation of unconditional love, one of the ways in which the Source reaches out to us and shows us transformational possibilities. They are a bridge between worlds, from the physical world around us to infinite worlds beyond. The more we flow with life, without trying to control it, the more we are able to recognize miracles. They bring new perceptions of what is real, offering guidance and affirmation. In a world of illusion, miracles are universal Blessings from the Divine. Experiencing them is transcendent.

Miracles are everywhere. They live in your perception, and exist only if you acknowledge them. So, open your heart and see the abundance of miracles that strew your path. They are manifestations of Divine love. Recognize them. Receive them. Let go of feelings of separation and isolation and connect to the Oneness of the All That Is. This is a portal to knowing miracles. Welcome miracles into your life. Understand that they are a natural part of your life. They are created through love, and through your love you will find them. Allow them to open you up to the power of healing, forgiveness and unconditional love. Enter into their Mystery. Let them bring you meaning, insight, and truth. Let miracles transform your life. Know that you are a miracle!

*"Miracles start to happen
when you give as much energy to your dreams as to your fears."*
Richard Wilkins, Australian television presenter


*"People usually consider walking on water or in thin air a miracle.
But I think the real miracle
is not to walk either on water or in thin air,
but to walk on earth.
Every day we are engaged in a miracle,
which we don't even recognize...
All is a miracle."*
Thich Nhat Hanh


*"Miracles are natural.
When they do not occur, something has gone wrong."*
A Course in Miracles [Channelled Source]


*"Look at the birth of a child.
How can you not believe in miracles?"*
Catherine Pulsifer, author and publisher of motivational words of wisdom


*"Don't demand miracles – notice them."*
Nirgun: Awakening Notes

# The Forty-Second Blessing

*I am blessed with silence -*

*- thank you for helping me to be in the silence of the universe*

As we open up to living in consciousness, we begin to realize how much we need silence. All our Blessings are offered to us in silence. But in our busy lives, we don't spend much time in silence. We may think, if we think about it at all, that we just don't have time. But the real reason is not a lack of time, but fear. Fear of being alone in the silence. Alone with ourselves. Fear of what we may find within; of what we may not find. So we distract ourselves with continuous sound: the radio, television, loud music, constant chattering with others. And the noise of the streets: the clamour of traffic, 'music' blaring from shops and cafes. Anything not to be alone in silence.

The Blessing of silence is a profound gift. Silence is not only an absence of sound, but a place of spiritual awakening and healing. The more time we spend in silence, the more it reveals its mysteries. Silence is a powerful guide on our journey and an instrument of spiritual evolvement. Rooted in silent awareness, we connect most profoundly to the power of Spirit, to our Higher Self and our intuition. Many insights may surface. In silence and stillness lie the wisdom of the heart, an open channel to the Source. And a shared silence with a partner or friend can be a powerful experience, offering a connection beyond words, a loving communion of the heart.

Receive this Blessing and spend time in silence. Silence is not just an escape from the madness of *maya,* the noise of the physical world. It is also a place of spiritual transformation. Be with yourself in the silence. Breathe deeply and slowly, fully present in the moment. Meditate, go for a walk in nature, or sit under a tree. And practise doing simple tasks in silence: washing the floor or preparing a meal. Silence speaks to us in many voices; it is a place of refuge, a place to gather strength, a place of healing and revelation and truth. Let the silence of the universe embrace you. Actually it is not silent at all, but filled with myriad sounds, audible only to the spiritual traveller. Audible through your soul, not your ears. Stay in the silent stillness of your heart. In the blessed silence of the universe, hear the wisdom of the Divine.

*"Silence will mirror for you that which you hide deep inside.*
*Silence is your greatest guide."*
Saint Germain & Ashamarae McNamara: The Blueprint of Oneness


*"Your vision will only become clear*
*when you look into the silence of your own heart.*
*Who looks outside, sleeps.*
*Who looks inside, awakes."*
Carl Jung: Memories, Dreams and Reflections


*"Al the evils in the world*
*derive from the fact that we are unable to sit quietly in a room."*
Blaise Pascal


*"Silence is the altar of Spirit."*
Paramahamsa Yogananda: Autobiography of a Yogi


*"Finally, I became silent, and began to listen.*
*I discovered in the silence, the voice of God."*
Soren Kierkegaard


*"Silence, holding the universe...*
*Perhaps that is the only religion: how we interpret the silence."*
Nomi Sharron: Then Let the Barrier Fall

# The Forty-Third Blessing

*I am blessed with help on my journey towards knowing myself -*
*- thank you for helping me along the way, to accept what I cannot know*

Many sages teach that the aim of spiritual practice is to know ourselves. But we cannot know ourselves. Our real Self is the Divine within; this is everything we are. But the truth of this will always elude us. Another spiritual paradox: that we must undertake the journey, although we know that we shall never arrive. So why start the journey? Firstly, it is an act of trust, essential to our spiritual being. And secondly, along the way we will learn invaluable lessons about ourselves, about the nature of consciousness, and about truth. We will find answers to questions we didn't know how to ask. The goal of spirituality is to journey in the right way, to trust the paradox of the path, and to gain insight into the journeyer.

Every step of the way we need to ask, who is the traveller? Who is this being that inhabits my body, that uses my mind, that feels my feelings? Who is the "my"? Who is asking these questions? We continue to ask because this is the path of the spiritual warrior, the seeker after truth. We are Spirit, and Spirit is unknowable. Our questing brings us closer to the Source, but the Source is unknowable. Opening ourselves up to receive the grace of God, to live in God consciousness, is all there is. Is all we are. Once we accept the paradox that we cannot know who we truly are, but we continue the journey, we may arrive at a sudden realization that who we are is simply presence. And that we have arrived at the beginning of our journey.

The journey to discover who you are must be undertaken in good faith, for its own sake. This is a journey within, to the deepest part of yourself. Be courageous! Look within, without expectation of finding the answers you seek. Continue to question. Ask yourself, who are you? You are not your body, nor your mind, nor your feelings. So who is the real you? Stand back and observe. Let go of all definitions of identity: gender, nationality, religion, culture, career, abilities. They may be convenient for you, but they are divisive, and cause separation. These things are part of you, but they are not who you are. Observe yourself, and be open to whatever appears. Accept yourself, as you find yourself. Your quest to know yourself may not answer the questions you ask. But it will be a portal to expanding consciousness, wisdom, and truth.

*"How little do we know that which we are!*
*How less what we may be!"*
Lord Byron: Don Juan


*"Knowing yourself is the beginning of all wisdom."*
Aristotle


*"We are each three people:*
*who we think we are,*
*whom others think we are,*
*and who we really are."*
Source Unknown


*"The aim of all spiritual practice is to know your real Self.*
*To know the knower."*
Swami Satchidananda: To Know Yourself


*"He who knows others is wise;*
*he who knows himself is Enlightened."*
Lao Tzu: The Way


*"In the silence I begin to rediscover who I am."*
Nomi Sharron: Paths to Spiritual Awakening

# The Forty-Fourth Blessing

*I am blessed with unconditional love -*
*- thank you for helping me to love myself unconditionally, and the Divine within all life*

Love is everything. It is not something we do, it is the essence of who we are. A state of being. Love is a direction, our journey and our awakening. The more that love embraces our journey, the more profound is our understanding of the way. We may feel that we were unloved by our parents, and spend the rest of our lives looking for unconditional love. But love is within us. As children, we were probably taught to "Love your neighbour as yourself". But we forget the second part – *as yourself.* First, we need to love ourselves, *as we are*, unconditionally. Only then, are we truly able to love others. Everything comes from love. The Bible, in both the Old Testament and the New, commands us to "Love the Lord your God…" Not obey; love.

Love is the manifestation of our spirituality: loving the Divine, loving ourselves, loving others. It is the highest vibrational state. All the evil in the world stems from our inability to truly love ourselves, and recognize our divinity. Perhaps we feel that we don't deserve love. But this is a fiction of the ego mind. Created in the image of God, we *are* love. Love has nothing to do with liking people; some people we may like more than others. But *love* is who we are. It asks nothing of other people, not even their love – if it does, it is neediness, not love – and is unaffected by the way that others behave towards us. Love is the ultimate healer. It can transform any situation. It is the expression of our Higher Self, our wholeness, our connection to the Divine. Love is the manifestation of our consciousness. As we move more deeply into consciousness, our love expands.

Love is the doorway to enlightenment. Go through the doorway. Let go of any residual judgementalness, blame, guilt, feelings of superiority or inferiority; the illusion of separation created by the ego. These are just 'indulgences' to protect us from our fears. Love is the opposite of fear. [Fear has many opposites!] Inhabit the love that is your being, and let it dispel your fears. Open yourself to be a channel to receive love: a Blessing from the Divine to you, and through you to others, and to the world. Unconditional love transforms unconditionally. It enables us to see miracles. Let everything you do be a manifestation of love. The energy of this love can change the world. You are the change you want to see. You are love.

*"Let us love one another, for love is from God."*
The New Testament, St Paul: Letter to the Romans

*"Love is the doorway to Enlightenment.*
*Love is Enlightenment."*
Orin [Channelled Source]

*"Only by loving God can we truly love ourselves."*
A course in Miracles [Channelled Source].

*"We are not held back by the love we didn't receive in the past,*
*but by the love we're not extending in the present."*
Marianne Williamson: A Return to Love

*"Love is all that exists; all else is illusion."*
Saint Germaine & Ashamarae McNamara: The Blueprint of Oneness

*"The longest journey is from the head to the heart.*
*And the shortest."*
Nomi Sharron: Paths to Spiritual Awakening

# The Forty-fifth Blessing

*I am blessed with gratitude -*
*- thank you for helping me live in gratitude for all that I am, all that I receive*

Expressing gratitude is a fundamental part of spiritual practice, a natural response to receiving the manifold Blessings showered upon us each day. Showing gratitude strengthens our connection to the Divine and to our Higher Self, and to the good within us. Living in gratitude is a manifestation of love: love for ourselves, and love for the Divine within us, and all around us. It is a deeply healing experience; it connects us to our integrity and wholeness. It reminds us of who we are meant to be, and what's important. The more we live in gratitude, the more we open ourselves to receive Blessings, and the more blessed we become. Manifesting gratitude, we experience most profoundly our connection to the Oneness of all, and know, in a knowing that is beyond words, that there is no separation.

Gratitude is a dedication of our life to God, a prayer, a hymn of praise, a song sung by a choir of angels, filling the universe with compassion and love. The Hebrew word for Blessing, 'bracha', comes from the same root as 'berech', a knee. When we bend our knee to the Divine in gratitude – literally or metaphorically – we connect more profoundly to our Higher Self and to our Blessings. Our heart opens and expands. Our compassion for ourselves, and for others, increases. The more we show gratitude, the more aware we become of all that we have to be grateful for, and the more we are able to receive what we didn't know we had been offered. Expressing gratitude strengthens our connection to our soul. It is transformative.

Show gratitude each day for the manifold Blessings that are showered upon you. This gives them form, and makes it easier for you to receive and experience them. Show gratitude to your family, your friends, your work colleagues; to your unseen guides who are always with you. Living in gratitude, you cannot feel judgementalness, self-righteousness or blame; you cannot feel isolated or alone. Embrace gratitude, and the abundance of your life. See everything through the lens of gratitude; this releases all feelings of lack and deprivation. Nourish and expand your heart; connect to the sacredness of the Source and the sacred within you. Gratitude is a profound expression of unconditional love. Receive and manifest this love, and share the abundance of your Blessings with others. Let gratitude open you up to receive grace. In gratitude, all your Blessings are manifest.

*"Gratitude is the memory of the heart."*
Jean Baptiste Massieu, born deaf in Paris in 1772, pioneering deaf educator


*"An attitude of gratitude*
*Is more than just a platitude*
*For in that place*
*Arises grace*
*Amazing in its latitude."*
Nick Bagnall: The Friend [Quaker publication]


*"A grateful heart is the beginning of greatness.*
*It is an expression of humility,*
*the foundation of prayer, faith, courage,*
*contentment, happiness and love."*
James E. Faust, American religious leader, lawyer and politician


*"It is not joy that makes us grateful.*
*It is gratitude that makes us joyful."*
Brother David Steindle-Rast, Benedictine monk, pioneer in interfaith dialogue


*"Let gratitude be the pillow upon which you kneel*
*to say your nightly prayer."*
Maya Angelou: Celebrations - Rituals of Peace and Prayer

# The Forty-Sixth Blessing

*I am blessed with humility -*
*- thank you for helping me to know my true worth, and so happily embrace humility*

Humility is a profound expression of our spirituality. It has nothing to do with humbleness, which is concerned with putting ourselves down and buying into 'victimhood'. Humility is the opposite of arrogance, not of self-belief. It is knowing our own true worth, and so not needing to trumpet it. We know that our feelings of self worth come from within. This liberates us from dependence upon other people's opinions, judgement, and approval of us. Humility is born of our unconditional love for ourselves, and a strong sense of self worth. It is *because* we have strong feelings of self worth that we are able to live in humility. It is the expression of our authentic Self, the true measure of our integrity, and our feelings of profound gratitude.

Humility brings us to another spiritual paradox: that we are both the centre of our world, and simultaneously an infinitesimal dot in the vastness of the cosmos. That everything we are and do *matters*, but the glory is not ours. This is simply the way things are. Humility shows us that we do not control our lives; that our Blessings are bestowed upon us by grace and come from a Higher Source. Knowing this, we may connect more deeply to the immutable laws of the All That Is, and to our rightful place within the scheme of things. Our task is to be open to receive our Blessings with gratitude and humility, and manifest them in the way we live our lives. In humility our soul meets its human incarnation. In humility, we know, profoundly, that all is well; that all shall be well. That all is well.

Living in true humility is the greatest manifestation of living in God consciousness. When we do this, we are the embodiment of our Higher Self, the Divine within us. Honour your humility, and the path you are walking. Acknowledge that you don't need other people's approval in order to live with self-esteem; nor will others' censure deflect you from your way. Celebrate your authentic self. Manifest all your Blessings as an expression of your gratitude and humility. Let them expand into the infinite; there are no boundaries. Let your humility bring you closer to the wisdom of the All That Is, which is supporting and sustaining you. Let the Oneness of the Source embrace you with tenderness, peace and infinite love. In your humility, be at peace with yourself, and an example to the world.

*"True humility, the basis of the Christian system,*
*is the low but deep, firm foundation of all virtues."*
Edmund Burke, 18th century British politician, philosopher and author


*"If serving is beneath you,*
*Leadership is beyond you."*
Anonymous


*"Be humble for you are made of earth.*
*Be noble for you are made of stars."*
Serbian Proverb


*"Humility, that low, sweet root*
*From which all heavenly virtues shoot."*
Thomas Moore, spiritual writer


*"There is something in humility which strangely exalts the heart."*
Saint Augustine


*"True humility is being open to receive both praise and blame*
*with equal gratitude."*
Nomi Sharron: Paths to Spiritual Awakening

# The Forty-Seventh Blessing

*I am blessed with forgiveness -*
*-thank you for helping me to forgive myself, and those whom I feel have wronged me*

Forgiveness is a profound Blessing, essential in our spiritual evolvement. It is born of unconditional love for ourselves and others. It liberates us from the tyranny of the past and from other people's power over us. We may feel that we cannot forgive others, but this is because we are stuck in our pain, or caught up in seeking justice, or possibly revenge. But it is not our job to judge. It is our job to forgive. Forgiveness is often misunderstood. It does *not* mean condoning uncharitable behaviour. But only by forgiving can we let go of the resentment or anger that we harbour towards those whom we feel have hurt us, and our investment in staying a victim. Forgiving someone is not about them. It is about us, part of our spiritual journey. Though it may also help to heal those whom we forgive.

Perhaps the hardest thing of all is to forgive ourselves. This is bound up with feelings of unworthiness; and with the mountain of guilt that most of us are carrying. Guilt comes from a lack of self-acceptance and self-love. It is a way of punishing ourselves, fed by pain or suppressed anger. Guilt keeps us stuck, the victim of our own judgementalness, unable to forgive ourselves. But we have a choice. So, see what is hiding behind your feelings of guilt. Examine the things within you that you think are unforgiveable. Learn from them, then start the process of letting go. Find that place of love within you, and choose to forgive yourself. You can! Forgiving yourself is one of the most important tasks of your journey. It is a mark of your spiritual growth.

Embrace your wisdom, your integrity, your compassion, and open your heart to forgiveness. Let go of guilt; live in unconditional love. There is no room for both. Cut the ropes that bind you to limited beliefs and fears. Forgive others, and liberate yourself by taking back your power from them, and reclaiming your autonomy. Forgive yourself, and expand the compassion of your heart. Create rituals of forgiveness, for others, and for yourself. Live in forgiveness consciousness. Let it be a portal to transformation for you, and for the world. Forgiveness brings with it sacred healing. But know that ultimately there is nothing to forgive. Although in order to realize this, you must experience the journey through forgiveness. In this spiritual paradox lie truth and ultimate freedom.

*"Father, forgive them, for they know not what they do."*
Jesus, on the cross, referring to his executioners


*"When I have forgiven myself, I remember who I am.*
*Then I am able to bless myself.*
*And then I can bless everyone else."*
A Course in Miracles [Channelled source]


*"True forgiveness is not an action after the fact;*
*it is the way you live each moment."*
David Ridge: The Art of Forgiveness


*"The practice of forgiveness is our most important contribution*
*to the healing of the world."*
Marianne Williamson: Return to Love


*"Forgiveness is the final form of love."*
Reinhold Niebuhr


*"To err is human; to forgive, divine."*
Alexander Pope: An Essay on Criticism

# The Forty-Eighth Blessing

*I am blessed with consciousness –*
*– thank you for helping me to grow into awakened consciousness*

We come into this life from a place of perfect consciousness. As we incarnate in human form, we lose the memory of our divinity. This life is a yearning back towards consciousness, to embrace what we have known but have forgotten. Consciousness is the final surrender of the unconscious ego mind, and the release of its control over our life. It is an awakening to live the Divine purpose of our life, allowing it to unfold in its own perfect way, even if we do not know what that is. Consciousness is knowing the Oneness of all beings, of all Creation; knowing that we are all held within universal love, with no separation. Consciousness sees the illusion of the physical world, and lives simultaneously in all dimensions.

Everything is born of consciousness. Everything *is* consciousness. Consciousness created the universe; the universe did not create consciousness. Consciousness embraces all dimensions of reality simultaneously. It is the unity that joins God the Divine with the Divine within each of us. Consciousness is meeting the Mystery at the heart of Spirit and letting it embrace us. It is sacred surrender, the ultimate merging of the self into universal energy, and the profound knowing that there is no separation. Consciousness is the heart of the universe beating in each breast; a web of prayer, mapping miracles, awakening the world from its slumber. It is presence, pure being, within which all knowing is held. Consciousness is the manifestation of unconditional love, breathing the universe. It embraces the journey that dissolves the ego into the soul, the soul into the God-Self, [Atman] and finally Atman into Spirit [Brahman].

In consciousness, all our Blessings are offered. Live in consciousness. Be consciousness. Journey towards knowing Spirit, while simultaneously being aware that the infiniteness of Spirit is unknowable. Consciousness is knowing, and not knowing, and being at peace with both. It is the ultimate acceptance of spiritual paradox. Let consciousness expand your capacity to receive and manifest and share your Blessings. Be a channel for the Divine, bringing light to you and to the world. Be in the limitlessness of consciousness. Allow it to expand your love, your compassion, your gratitude and humility. Consciousness is the revelation of your soul; the Divine presence within you and within the All That Is. Consciousness is everything. It is your journeying, and your homecoming, and your home.

*"Consciousness is simply regaining our memory."*
Osho: The Book of Wisdom


*"There is one unity, one unified wholeness, total natural law,*
*in the transcendental unified consciousness."*
Maharishi Mahesh Yogi


*"Mind is consciousness which has put on limitations.*
*You are originally unlimited and perfect consciousness."*
Bhagavan Sri Ramana Maharshi


*"Atman [individual consciousness] and Brahman [universal consciousness]*
*are one."*
Hindu scriptures


*"Consciousness is the key and the doorway...*
*Soul journeys guided through infinity*
*Truth on the ragged tongue of the wind...*
*Consciousness is meeting with Mystery*
*Transformation*
*Our journeying*
*And our homecoming*
*And our home.*
*Consciousness is          "*
Nomi Sharron: From the poem Consciousness

# The Forty-Ninth Blessing

*I am blessed with surrender -*

*- thank you for helping me to surrender to Divine will*

To reach the Blessing of surrender is both the goal of our spiritual journey, and the way we travel; surrendering our personal will to the will of the Divine. Another spiritual paradox: how does surrender equate with taking responsibility for our life? But we can hold truth in our heart, though we may not understand it with our head. Surrender is not the same as resignation, which is being a victim of circumstance. Rather, it is a conscious choice. In surrendering to Divine will for our life, we exercise our ultimate free choice: to allow our life to unfold in its own unique way. In surrender, we welcome the unknown, in all its mystery. The act of surrender is born of consciousness, unconditional love, acceptance and trust.

Surrender is the manifestation of the yearning of the soul to be reunited with the All That Is. On this human journey, the ego creates separation from the Source. This is the cause of all suffering and misery. Surrender is giving up our agenda for our life, our assumptions and expectations, our attachment to past and future; and above all, it is the death of the ego, thus allowing us to merge with the whole, to become inseparable from the universal flow of life. It is our conscious transformation into the manifestation of our eternal Self, beyond the limitations of ego, body and mind. It is trusting Divine will to guide our life to be a blossoming of consciousness and unconditional love. It is the infinite trust that leads us to the merging of ourselves with the boundless, the individual with the All That Is, the human with the Divine.

Surrender irrevocably the idea of separation from the Source, created by your ego. Relinquish your struggle to control. Let your life be guided by Divine will, although you may not know its purpose. Connect to your deepest wisdom and accept the flow of life. Allow yourself to touch the profound Mystery of the All That Is. Remind yourself, again and again, that we are all held in the same Oneness; there is no separation. Surrender your personal will, and join your power to universal energy. This is truly empowering! Inhabit love, the Source of everything, the Divine manifest within you, and within the All That Is. Let surrender bring profound meaning to your life; transcendence, wholeness, peace, and bliss. Through surrender, you may receive and manifest all your Blessings.

*"Thy will be done."*
The Lord's Prayer: The Anglican Book of Common Prayer


*"Nothing real can be threatened.*
*Nothing unreal exists.*
*Herein lies the peace of God."*
A Course in Miracles [Channelled Source]


*"Surrender involves getting out of our own way*
*and living in accord with a higher will,*
*expressed as the wisdom of the heart."*
Dan Millman: The Laws of Spirit


*"You have to let go of the life you planned*
*in order to live the life that God has planned."*
Pastor John Hagee


*"Life is God's novel; let God write it."*
Isaac Bashevis Singer


*"Just when the caterpillar thought it was the end of the world,*
*it became a butterfly."*
Source Unknown

# The Fiftieth Blessing

*I am blessed with freedom –*
  *– thank you for helping me to accept what is, and live in expanding freedom*

Freedom is the ultimate expression of living in consciousness. We are born free, but our freedom is curtailed often by parental and societal norms. Our human journey, and the journey through these Blessings, leads us towards the freedom we have lost. Freedom has nothing to do with external circumstances; indeed, it is our egoic identification with the outside world that prevents us from living in freedom. Freedom is a state of being, born in consciousness and unconditional love. It is independent of our physical circumstances and the 'reality' around us. A prisoner may be freer than a prison guard, a pauper freer than a king. Real freedom, like the hand that draws itself in an Escher painting, is the freedom to choose freedom.

Freedom presents us with another spiritual paradox: that only by accepting what is, and surrendering to Divine will, can we have real freedom. And, like all spiritual paradoxes, it is profoundly true. For only by accepting what is, and letting go of the control of the ego mind, can we make conscious choices, and choose how we respond to what is. Freedom is both freedom *from*, and freedom *to*; freedom from: the rule of our emotions [anxiety, anger, resentment, guilt, fear] and all the false perceptions of the ego mind; and freedom to: live unbounded, in each present moment, in consciousness, taking full responsibility for our choices. Freedom is the road we walk from the bondage of attachment to the realization of limitless choice. Trusting the flow of life is not a limitation of freedom, but an expansion of infinite possibilities. Nothing and no-one owns you, nor limits you, nor controls you. Freedom is not so much free choice in any particular circumstance, as liberated life!

Freedom is the goal and the journey of your awakening consciousness, a manifestation of both your surrender and your spiritual yearning. It is the liberation of your heart from the tyranny of your ego mind. You have let go of your conditioned beliefs, assumptions, judgementalness, guilt; the film of your life buzzing in your head. Congratulate yourself and celebrate! Be empowered, and choose the reality you want to create. Accept what is, live in the moment, be open to receive all that the universe offers you. Remind yourself that you are free to make choices in every moment. Make choices that are born in the clarity of consciousness, that come from your integrity, your wholeness, your heart. Live your freedom, and dance in the limitless perfection of the infinite, the eternal, the Divine. This is freedom with a cosmic smile!

*"Man is born free, but everywhere he is in chains."*
Jean Jacques Rousseau: The Social Contract

*"The greatest freedom is to be responsible."*
Lazaris [Channelled Source]

*"We are truly free when we own nothing."*
Vaswani, walking as a Sadhu

*"We who lived in the concentration camps*
*can remember the men who comforted others,*
*giving away their last piece of bread...*
*Sufficient proof that everything can be taken away*
*except the last human freedom –*
*to choose one's attitude in any circumstances."*
Victor Frankl: Man's Search for Meaning

*"The Truth shall make you free."*
Jesus: The New Testament, John, Chapter 8, verse 31

# The Fifty-First Blessing

*I am blessed with prayer -*

*- thank you for helping me to know that my life is a prayer*

The power of prayer for human transformation lies at the heart of spirituality. Prayer is a manifestation of our consciousness, a transformative meeting with God. God does not need our prayers; we do. Prayer opens us up to a deepening knowing of the Divine. It is our acknowledgement of living in companionship with God's presence, reminding ourselves that we are always held in God's love. Prayer is an act of profound gratitude, for all that we are, for all that we are given: the infinite Blessings showered upon us; those that we know, and those that are offered that we have not yet received. The more we acknowledge our Blessings in prayer, the more we open ourselves up to receive. And our prayers are always answered, though not necessarily in the way we may expect!

There are three levels of prayer: the petitionary, asking God for things; the conversational, having a dialogue with God; and the contemplative. All our prayers bring us closer to God, but only contemplative prayer is our ultimate surrender to God. In Hebrew, the verb to pray, 'lehitpalel', is reflexive, containing within it the concept of looking inward, examining our own soul. It is an affirmation of our being in God consciousness. Prayer is also a source of healing, not because we ask God to cure our sickness, but because prayer opens us up to receive healing. Prayer is an expression both of our yearning to live in God consciousness, and a manifestation of our surrender to Divine will. Prayer expands our consciousness, linking our earthly existence with the celestial realms. It is a medium of revelation, an affirmation of miracles. When offered in devotion, everything we do is a prayer.

Prayer is an expression of your deepening relationship with God; and with yourself. The power of prayer is in the *intention* with which it is offered. Create a ritual of prayer that is meaningful to you, and practise it daily. Your prayers may be in words, in song, in dance, chanting, being in nature; anything that brings you into awakened consciousness. And of course your prayers may be in silence, the silence itself becoming the power of the prayer. Come to your prayers with devotion, offering God your humility, your vulnerability, your gratitude, and your love. Let prayer expand your compassion and your love. And remember others in your prayers; those whom you know personally, and those you don't, who will be blessed by your prayers. Make prayers for healing the world, sending light and love, harmony and peace out into the universe. Your life is a prayer.

*"You carry Mother Earth within you...*
*And in that insight of inter-being,*
*it is possible to have real communication with the Earth,*
*which is the highest form of prayer."*
Thich Nhat Hanh


*"Prayer is an act of love; words are not needed.*
*All that is needed is the will to love."*
Saint Teresa of Avila


*"Prayer is the longing of the soul for communion with God."*
Mahatma Gandhi


*"Everything you do is a prayer,*
*when you smile that is a prayer -*
*when you walk that is a prayer -*
*when you give someone a kiss that is a prayer...*
*when you laugh, when you dance,*
*everything you do is a prayer..."*
*Lee Hall: Spoonface Steinberg,*
*[Spoken by the eponymous heroine, a little girl, autistic, with terminal cancer]*


*"If the only prayer you say in your whole life is 'Thank you',*
*that is enough."*
Meister Eckhart

# The Fifty-Second Blessing

*I am blessed with the revelation of the Divine within me –*

*- thank you*

We are all created in the image of God, and God is within each of us. Inhabiting the Divine within us transforms our life, letting us transcend the illusions of the physical world, and enter the Mystery at the heart of the All That Is. Through gratitude, surrender, love, and prayer, we reaffirm the Divine within and open ourselves up to receive its guidance. As we connect more profoundly to the Divine, we move more deeply into our own inner wisdom. God within us is our spiritual centre, out of which all things are formed. By living in God consciousness, we are able to embrace uncertainty and not knowing, and trust that we may receive what we do not understand. We open ourselves up as a channel for guidance and wisdom. A sacred mission.

God is everything, and God is within us, and we are within the divinity of God. Our oneness with the Divine simply *is*. It doesn't change, or even deepen; what may change is our perception of it. Consciousness is our awareness of the Divine within us, the divinity of the All That Is, and the Oneness of all. In God consciousness we manifest the ultimate realization of non-separation. It is this conscious knowing that transforms our lives, and vanquishes forever the reign of our ego, enabling the birth of the Self to manifest in the unity of the All That Is. And actually, as you embrace your spiritual Self with expanding consciousness, you realize that there is no journey, for you are already 'there'. There is no goal, for the goal is the way. And the way is manifesting the revelation of God within you: the way you open up to the wisdom of your heart and *live* the truth you find there.

This is living in God consciousness. Christ consciousness. Buddha consciousness. They are all one. There is no separation. Know this. Be the knowing. All your Blessings are held in your recognition of Divine revelation within you. Receive your Blessings and allow your life to unfold according to Divine will. The Divine within is the light of enlightenment. Enlightenment is not a destination; it is the expansion of your consciousness, which sees the sacred within everything. Enlightenment is love. And love is who you are. It is the doorway to enlightenment. Live your life as though it is a path towards enlightenment, but know that we do not 'reach' enlightenment. Rather, it may reach us. Your task is simply to open your heart to God and be ready to receive. And then wait for grace.

*And God said:*
*"I AM THAT I AM"* *
The Old Testament: Exodus 3, verse 14


And *we* are what we are.


We are
THAT


So simple
So profound

125

# The Joker

The Joker comes to remind us that living in spiritual consciousness is serious, challenging, perhaps formidable, and may appear at times to be daunting, or even scary. But it is not earnest. The Joker's role is to help us to let go of our 'earnest' concerns and occupations, our heavy mood when we take ourselves too seriously, or get tangled up in the dramas we create. Spirituality demands the whole of us: our integrity, our trust, our courage, our passion and compassion, our gratitude, humility, and love. But it also asks that we take ourselves lightly. The Joker blesses us with the gift of lightness [the linguistic connection among light, lightness, delight and enlightenment is not random!]. It shows us how to skip through a dark forest or splash in the rain; to sing and dance and run with joy; to soar. Taking ourselves lightly imbues us with light and helps us to spread light around us.

As children, it is natural to play. Our play expresses our curiosity, our imagination, our spontaneity and creativity; the sheer joy of being alive in the moment. Our play created a whole world, of magic and miracles and mystery. The Joker reminds us to reconnect to this wondrous world of the playfulness and fun of our inner child; of imagination and lust for life; of exploring wherever this takes us, and enjoying *not* being sensible. The Joker is the 'trickster' in the pack, playing jokes on us to show us the humour in our lives, to get us to laugh at ourselves when nothing else can get us out of the dramas we dig ourselves into. And the Joker, of course, is within each of us, bursting to get out and laugh at our foibles!

Spirituality is not about suffering in order to achieve something, however much this was part of your conditioning. So give yourself permission to take yourself lightly. Connect to your Joker within. Do things that you enjoy – for no reason, just because you enjoy doing them. Reconnect to your inner child and live fully in the moment. Laugh at the dramas you create, at how much importance you place on trivialities. Inhabit your wild side: paint a wall in your bedroom in rainbow colours, jump in puddles in the rain, stand in the middle of a field at night and shout "yes" to the universe. Yes, to a life that manifests all of who you are: lightness and laughter, curiosity and creativity, playfulness and fun. Yes!

The Joker comes to help us take ourselves **light**ly –
and see the **light** and **light**ness and de**light** in en**light**enment!

Note:
If the Joker appears in a divinatory spread, take heed!
It has come to remind you
that you are taking yourself too seriously.
So put aside whatever challenges
you feel you are facing at the moment,
and enter your inner child's sense of playfulness and fun
– now!


You can also *choose* the Joker!
The Joker is a good choice
if you feel you are becoming entrenched in challenges
and do not see your way forward.
Often, the way forward – is sideways.
So step aside,
detach yourself from your dramas,
and allow the Joker into your life, big time.

The Joker will sort you out!

# Guided Meditation / Visualization

Before going on the Guided Meditation, you might like to acquire the Blessing Cards.
They are intended as an integral part of your Blessing journey,
and if used with correct intention, will greatly enhance it.
For details, see below ***

On this meditation, we shall connect to a particular Blessing.
Before you embark upon this journey, you may choose a Blessing to take with you.
Or you may ask for guidance for a Blessing in a Divinatory Spread.
[You will need Blessing cards to do this.]
Memorize both parts of the Blessing you are taking with you.
Or you can wait to be given your Blessing on the journey.
The journey of this visualization has profound symbolic meaning.

Please note that in order to obviate the frequent use of he / she, him / her, the feminine form has been used for the child who appears in this visualization. If you are male, please substitute appropriately!

Sit in a quiet place where you won't be disturbed or distracted. Sit comfortably with your legs uncrossed and your feet firmly on the ground. Take off your shoes and connect more closely to the ground. Or sit on the floor if this is comfortable for you, cross-legged, with your back upright. Relax and quieten your mind. Close your eyes, and feel your body in contact with the chair, or the floor. [You may do this meditation lying down, but make sure you don't fall asleep!] Relax completely. Go through each part of your body, tensing and relaxing each muscle in turn: your toes, feet, ankles, calf muscles, shins, knees, thighs, buttocks, pelvic area, groin, stomach, lower back, chest, upper back and shoulders, fingers, hands, forearms, upper arms, neck muscles, the back and top of your head, your face – eyes, nose, ears, mouth, cheeks; your jaw, which often holds a great deal of tension. Open your mouth and move your jaw from side to side, tensing and then relaxing it. Now feel your body, totally relaxed, sinking more and more deeply into the chair or the floor.

Concentrate on breathing slowly and rhythmically and watch your breath. Now take three deep healing breaths, breathing in from the tips of your toes, bringing the breath slowly up through your body to the crown of your head. As you breathe in, visualize a healing white light entering your body through your toes and moving up to the crown of your head. Hold the breath for a count of five, then breath out all the stress and stuck energy in your body. Do this again, with the second breath, breathing in from the tips of your toes, bringing the breath slowly through your body to the crown of your head, and visualize the healing white light moving up through your body. Hold the breath for a count of five, then breathe out all the pain and stress in your body. Take a third healing breath, breathing in from the tips of your toes, and visualize the healing white light moving up through your body as you bring the breath slowly up to the crown of your head. Hold the breath for a count of five, then exhale, letting out all the pain and stale energy in your body. Continue to breathe slowly and deeply, feeling calm and centred. Be aware of your breath.

Now gently slow your breathing and relax. Watch the slow, rhythmic flow of your breath, breathing in and breathing out. Empty your mind of thoughts. If thoughts come into your mind, as they will, just watch them, and let them go. Don't actively chase them away; this engages with them. Just watch them float away. If your mind tries to trick you by sneaking in more thoughts, be aware that that's exactly what it's doing – trying to trick you! Just observe the thoughts and let them go. Bring your focus back to your breathing, breathing slowly and rhythmically, in and out. Your body is now deeply relaxed. Your mind is quiet. You feel completely calm and still.

Now you are going on a journey. Ahead of you, you see a forest. It's dark and a little frightening, but something drives you on and you enter the forest. You go more deeply into the forest, making your way with some difficulty through the density of the trees. As you continue further and further into the forest, it becomes darker and more menacing. You can barely see your way forward. You feel very alone and very afraid. Afraid of the darkness, afraid of stumbling over obstacles on the way, afraid of what you might discover. But you are courageous, and you're determined to continue.

Gradually, the trees begin to thin out. It becomes lighter, less menacing. You find yourself on the other side of the forest. Now the forest, the darkness and the fear are behind you. You come out into a beautiful meadow. It's a bright sunny day, and you feel warm and safe, totally at ease. You lie down on the grass, letting the beauty of nature seep into your being. The scent of spring flowers wafts on the air, birds swoop and soar and coo gently in the trees; you feel all of nature smiling on you.

Suddenly you see a small child on the other side of the meadow. She / he is running towards you and calling your name. The child reaches you. This is your inner child. You tell her how pleased you are that she has come. She takes your hand and leads you across the meadow to a little stream. As you walk along the banks of the stream together, it opens out into a small river. The child jumps into the water and starts to laugh, a joyous infectious laugh, and you laugh too. She beckons to you, and you also jump into the water. You splash each other and laugh and have a lot of fun together. Then you notice that the river is flowing with Blessings. The child bends down and gathers up a Blessing. You get out of the water and sit together on the riverbank. The child gives you the Blessing. This is the Blessing that you have chosen for your journey today.

This is the Blessing you have brought with you, which the child symbolically gives you from the river. Or, if you prefer, the child will 'choose' a Blessing for you from the river. In this case, receive the Blessing from the child and meditate upon it until it becomes clear which Blessing you have been given. Then find your own words for the Blessing. Start with the words, "I am blessed with…" And the second part with the words, "Thank you for helping me to…" Either way, focus on the help you would like in manifesting this Blessing. Welcome it with love.

Lying down by the river, with the little child next to you, you feel the warm sun on your body, a gentle breeze wafting over you. You are totally relaxed, totally calm, at peace with yourself and the world. You have let go of everything that isn't part of this peace. Now say the first part of the Blessing: **"I am blessed with …"** Then add the words of the first part of whichever Blessing you have chosen. Allow the energy of the Blessing to seep into you. Repeat the first half of your Blessing, **"I am blessed with ..."** Over and over: **"I am blessed with ..."**

Bring your attention into your heart, not your head. Breathe slowly and deeply, breathing in and breathing out. Move deeply within. Open up to receive the energy of the Blessing. Allow it to connect to your heart. Stay in your heart, and gently meditate upon these questions: Why have you chosen this particular Blessing? How does this Blessing manifest itself in your life? How would you *like* it to be manifest? In which ways does it resonate for you? How can this Blessing further enhance your life? Say the first part of the Blessing again: **"I am blessed with ..."** Over and over: **"I am blessed with ..."** Focus on receiving the Blessing here, now, in this present moment. Let it embrace you, with perfect love. You are blessed *now*.

Lying by the river, with the sun on your face, feel connected to the perfect harmony and stillness around you. Focus on your breath, on moving more deeply within. Don't be afraid to visit this inner place. It is your place of deepest knowing; of wisdom, and sanctuary; your Higher Self. It exists only for you. It is the place in you where the Divine resides. It is home.

You are deeply relaxed, calm and peaceful. Your heart is open. Be aware of each in breath, feel it expand your heart. Welcome whatever feelings or sensations come up for you, even if they seem bizarre or incomprehensible. Don't judge. These are voices from your Higher Self which can guide you, better than you know. Later, on further reflection, they will make more sense to you. You're going to stay here for a while, in this special place by the river. Stay in your heart, in the Blessing that you've chosen. Allow the energy of the Blessing to embrace you. Be in this moment, slowly breathing in and breathing out. Be in the stillness, in the peace.

**PAUSE.**

When you feel ready, move on to the second part of the Blessing. Say the words at the beginning of the second part: **"Thank you for helping me to …"** You are acknowledging the help and support you receive, and showing gratitude to the Giver of all Blessings. Gratitude expands your heart and brings you closer to the Divine energy of the Source. Repeat the words: **"Thank you for helping me to …"** Focus on this Blessing, on the help you need to let go of whatever is keeping you stuck, fearful, closed; anything that is preventing you from opening up and moving forward on your journey. Ask for the help you need to manifest this Blessing; to allow the energy of change and light to flow through you. Trust what emerges; it is the help you have asked for. Gradually, changes in your consciousness will come about. Allow them into your life. Remember, everything you need for growth and change is inside you, and will emerge for you when you are ready to receive it.

Again, focus on your breathing. Now bring your attention back to today's Blessing. Repeat both parts. **"I am blessed with … Thank you for helping me to … "** Bring this Blessing into your heart. Acknowledge that this is where it lives, that you will bring it back with you into your day.

When you feel ready, take the little child's hand. She will lead you back across the meadow. Say goodbye to the river flowing with Blessings, knowing that you can return to it any time you wish. Still holding the little child's hand, cross the meadow. Thank her for taking you to the river of Blessings and staying with you on your journey. Tell her – your inner child – that she is always in your heart. Watch her go, with love.

When you reach the edge of the forest, you notice that it is light and not at all frightening. You walk back across the forest with a spring in your step. Now there are no obstacles in your way. The trees that before had seemed terrifying are now friendly. The sun is shining. Birds that you had not noticed before are chirping in the trees. You walk back through the forest with gratitude and joy in your heart. As you leave the forest behind you, say again the whole of your Blessing: **"I am blessed with … Thank you for helping me to … "** Bring this Blessing back with you into the rest of your day. The rest of your life.

When you are ready, slowly open your eyes and come back into the room. Have a big stretch, and smile. Embrace the feeling of being very blessed!

Note down any feelings that came to you during the visualization. And any thoughts that you have now. Don't edit them! The thoughts that are sparked by your journey that may have the most profound effect on your life, often don't make any sense at first. So, jot down whatever comes into your mind, without censoring. Come back to your notes over the next days and weeks. Seemingly random thoughts are often triggers that affect the most profound spiritual growth.

Tune in to the balance and harmony of the universe,
be in the stillness and silence,
connect to the All That is,
receive your Blessings,
and transform your life.

Now you might like to say something like the following:
[or feel free to say your own words].

"Thank you for helping me
to recognize, receive, manifest, and share
all my Blessings."


You are the light.
You are the mirror
that shines forth the light.

*** The Blessing Cards are available in a beautiful Box Set, with a special instruction booklet giving
guidance on the many ways to use them.
For details, please contact: nomisharron@btinternet.com

# Epilogue

As you have opened up to receive your Blessings, you will have allowed yourself to connect more profoundly to your authentic Self. As you journey through the Blessings, you let go of the chains of your perceived limitations. You live more fully in the present moment, and move closer to the longings of your heart and soul. As you manifest expanding gratitude for your Blessings, you reach a deeper spiritual knowing, and attract ever more Blessings to you. Like attracts like; that is spiritual lore. Your growing consciousness is a portal to experiencing greater wholeness, love, freedom, joy and peace.

As you awaken each morning and bless your day, you open yourself up to receive guidance on your journey, a more profound atunement to your spirituality, a deepening wisdom of the power of being fully present in the moment. Manifesting your Blessings can transform you, and your life. You can bring further blessing into your life by blessing special occasions: a birthday, an anniversary, blessing your home or your place of work, celebrating the New Moon. Blessing your food before you eat is an important part of spiritual practice: blessing Mother Earth for nourishing you and providing your food, blessing those who harvest and gather it, and those who transport it. Blessing your food brings you into conscious alignment with the energy of the Source, and transforms your meal into a sacred rite. And blessing food together with others can strengthen the bonds of friendship and feelings of unity and oneness.

Each time you revisit the Blessings, you may reveal more of their mystery and meaning. On the Jewish festival of Simchat Torah, the Rejoicing of the Law, the last chapter of the last book of the Five Books of Moses is read out, followed immediately by the opening words of the first chapter of Genesis: "In the beginning…" So, too, the gift of the Blessings is circular, the end is followed by the beginning. As we end one cycle, we are led to the beginning of another…

Each Blessing you receive is a mirror of who you are, the best of who you are. Manifesting your Blessings in your daily life gives powerful fuel to your spiritual journey, a reminder of your connection to your Higher Self, and to the All That Is. As you celebrate your Blessings, you become a Blessing, for yourself, for those who know you, and for the world.

Now, in your Blessings, bless others. By blessing others, you reflect back to them their goodness, their wholeness, their compassion, and so strengthen these qualities within them. Bless everyone who is in your life. Bless people that you meet, even fleetingly: the bus driver, the shop assistant, the post office clerk. And bless those who may be angry or aggressive towards you. Remind yourself that their anger or aggression belongs to them, that it is not personal and you are not the cause, although it may also have something to teach you. Blessing someone who is angry is also a marker on your spiritual journey, showing that you no longer get caught up in other people's agendas. Your Blessing may also help them, even if they are not aware of it.

Expand your blessing of others by including people around the world whom you may not know personally, who are in distress. Bless world leaders and others in positions of authority, to make wise and compassionate decisions. Send Blessings of peace to warmongers, and love to those who show hatred towards others. By recognizing that there is a Divine spark within everyone, you can touch the unmanifest goodness within them, and so help to awaken it. We are each more than we seem.

Life itself is a Blessing. When we bless life, we connect to the Divine within ourselves, to a sense of belonging to the Oneness of the All That Is. Our lives become strengthened, more loving and compassionate, more meaningful and whole. All Blessings are a gift from the Creator. As you bless, you become a channel for spreading Divine love. You may not be known in the world, or acknowledged for what you do. But your presence reaches out to others, and blesses them. Your Blessings spread light and love and joy.

Just by being who you are, you are a Blessing, to yourself, to others, and to the world.

*"What lies behind us,*
*and what lies before us,*
*are tiny matters*
*compared to what lies within us."*
Ralph Waldo Emerson

# Affirmations

The process of receiving and manifesting our Blessings is continuous and circular.
Here are some affirmations for your onward journey:

Each day I receive, honour and celebrate my Blessings.
Each day I bless everyone who touches my life.
Each day I bless strangers who cross my path.
Each day I bless those who are suffering in the world.
Each day I bless Mother Earth and all of nature.
Each day I bless the Divine within everything.

I am a Blessing to myself.
I am a Blessing to others.
I am a Blessing to the world.

I am blessed.

Remember who you are, and whence you came.
All your Blessings are held in this remembrance...

Note: These Blessings are only a tiny part of the rich gifts with which you are blessed. As you connect more deeply to your Blessings, and blessing becomes an integral part of your life, you might like to add your own Blessings. You could make Blessing cards for them and add your own lines to these: "I am blessed with … Thank you for helping me to …" Your Blessings are infinite; you have only to awaken them.

*"You stand ready,*
*humanity has been waiting for you,*
*go forth and shine!"*
Saint Germain & Ashamarae McNamara:
The Blueprint of Oneness

Printed in the United States
By Bookmasters